SAVE HARMLESS AGREEMENT

MODEL PETROL ENGINES
PLUS
THE ATOM MINOR MARK III

www.KnowledgePublications.com

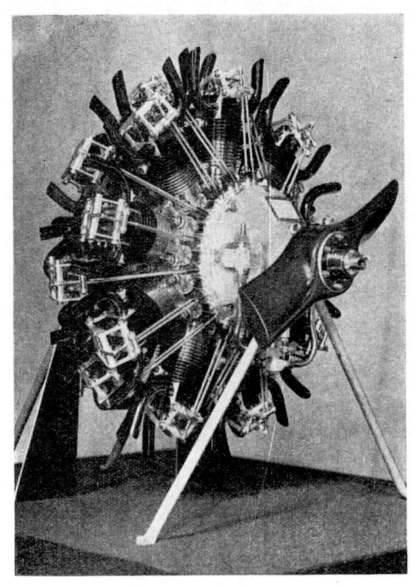

An eighteen-cylinder radial aircraft engine by
Mr. Gerald Smith, of Nuneaton

MODEL PETROL ENGINES

THEIR DESIGN, CONSTRUCTION AND USE

by

Edgar T. Westbury

*Associate Editor
of "The Model Engineer"*

PERCIVAL MARSHALL & CO., LTD.
23, Great Queen Street, London, W.C.2.

ISBN: 978-1-60322-042-2

www.KnowledgePublications.com

CONTENTS

PREFACE

THE object of this book may be stated in a very few words ; it is simply to assist readers to produce model petrol engines. Whether one wishes to start from first principles, and design the engines throughout, or to construct engines to well-tried designs which have been proved successful (and suitable for production with the average model engineer's equipment and facilities), it is believed that this book will prove helpful. It contains not only general information on the design of engines and their necessary appurtenances, but also a number of complete designs, of widely diverse types of engines, for practically every model engineering requirement.

Little is said of the commercially-produced engines which have for some years now been popular for model aircraft and similar purposes. This is not because of any prejudice against such engines, which fill a very useful and indeed essential place in the model engineering world, by enabling those who have no facilities for engine construction to enjoy the pleasures of running and handling these fascinating engines, and apply them to the propulsion of equally fascinating models. But the user of a ready-made engine can never experience the thrill which is felt by the creator of even the humblest engine which runs under its own power. The ready-made engine is a means—often an excellent and efficient means—to an end ; the amateur-built engine is an end in itself.

Nevertheless, much of the advice on running, maintaining and tuning engines is applicable equally to engines produced in a factory as to those built in the home workshop, and will be found useful to all users of small engines.

The model petrol engine deserves the attention of every progressive model engineer, because it provides scope for the very highest qualities of the designer and craftsman. Accuracy, both of the mind and hand, are essential to its production, and slipshod thinking or execution are alike fatal to its success. There is no type of small engine which better reflects the care and skill of the producer in its ultimate results ; the petrol engine is the most efficient of all prime movers in a small size, and can be applied successfully to practically every small power requirement. It is, perhaps, less spectacular than some other types of engines, and may attract less attention on the exhibition stand ; but even in this sphere notable successes have fallen to its lot, and the constructor who studies form and beauty in engine design can find many types of petrol or other internal combustion engines worthy of his attention. It has been said that the usual small petrol engine is not a true model ; this may provide a field for terminological dispute, but in one aspect of the use of models, namely experimental research, the small petrol engine can be, and has been, very usefully applied.

This book follows up an earlier *Model Engineer* handbook on Model Petrol Engines, which served a very useful purpose in the pioneer days, but has now been superseded by the rapid advance in both the design and popularity of these engines. For some years now, there has been a demand for up-to-date literature on this subject, which, it is hoped, this book will help to satisfy.

Popular movements always provide a happy hunting ground for the poseur and the charlatan, and the development of the model petrol engine has not been entirely immune from certain " growing pains " brought about by a surfeit of experts, some of whom aspire to be leaders of thought on the strength of a mere nodding acquaintance with a limited range of engines. The writer claims no right to the title of an ultimate authority on what is still an undeveloped and inexact science, but offers the results of 25 years of practical experience with almost every known type of model petrol engine, for the guidance of readers. During the period mentioned, a great deal of practical research has been undertaken in the basic principles of engine design, carburation, lubrication, ignition and other essential functions. For the last 20 years, articles dealing with these matters have been contributed regularly to *The Model Engineer*, and this material has been used as a nucleus for the contents of this book.

While the necessity for giving the reader the results of first-hand knowledge and experience will be apparent, and for this reason most of the designs shown in this book are the original work of the writer, some very interesting examples, both of design and construction, produced by friends and colleagues, are also included. Due acknowledgments are made for the assistance and co-operation of many model petrol engine enthusiasts, and without making any invidious distinctions, the names of Mr. D. H. Chaddock, B.Sc., Mr. Ian Bradley and the late Mr. F. Ford deserve mention for services in connection with the development and testing of engines.

Theoretical data may appear to be very meagre in this book, but the fact is that little *exact* information on factors which can be used as a basis for the design of small engines has yet been accumulated. The fundamental principles of internal combustion engines are, of course, the same, irrespective of size or type, and have been fairly exhaustively explored many years ago ; but the exact application of those principles to produce the efficiency of the modern engine, as employed in full-sized practice, has been possible only by long research and experiment, which are believed to be equally necessary in developing model engines. Without being dogmatic on the point, the writer expresses some doubt about the possibility of being able to design model petrol engines " off the slide rule," or by the application of any formulae so far available. Theory, in the true sense of the term—that is, a comprehensive, and as near as possible exact, knowledge of the mechanical and physical laws which underlie the working principles of an engine—is absolutely necessary to successful design ; but mathematical calculation is another thing altogether, and can only be used to apply the results of very carefully observed and recorded practical experiment. In any case, theory must always be used to assist and supplement practice, not to supersede it ; and the most brilliant logic and reasoning fails if it is not kept very closely in touch with facts.

CHAPTER I

THE REALM OF THE MODEL PETROL ENGINE

PRESENT-DAY model engineering offers almost unlimited scope for the application of model petrol engines in their various forms, and it may justly be claimed that the development of certain types of models is almost entirely dependent on the use of this form of motive power. Although petrol engines have been made in model form almost as long as their prototypes in full-sized practice, and there have been some very notable examples of successful model engines dating back as far as the early years of this century, it is only within recent years that they have been really popular, and that their special advantages have been properly demonstrated. At present, there are three main purposes for which model petrol engines are employed, and in two of them, at least, they may be said to be without a serious rival ; these are, in model power boats, aircraft and racing cars. But these applications by no means exhaust their possibilities, as it has been shown that they can be successfully adapted to model road and rail traction in all its forms ; and for very many years miniature engines which come legitimately within the category of models have been used for stationary power purposes, including the generation of electricity on a small scale, and pumping water for domestic and other purposes. In the latter respects, it can be shown that the model petrol engine has real practical utility, and can be designed to work with complete reliability, to say nothing of a running economy which surpasses that of any other small motive power.

1

Marine Engines

The first serious attempts at systematic use and development of model petrol engines must be credited to the model power boat fraternity, who have used such engines for the propulsion of all classes of water craft, including " prototype " motor liners, cargo boats, tugs and launches, and also racing hydroplanes. An attempt was made to commercialise model petrol engines for boat work in the first decade of this century by Mr. W. J. Smith, who produced the " Belvedere " engines, the quality and reliability of which were renowned to such an extent that the name became inseparably attached to their creator, who goes down to history as " Belvedere Smith." In 1924 a considerable impetus was given to the development of model petrol engines for boat propulsion by the establishment of the Model Power Boat Association International Trophy, for the best speed attained by a boat propelled by this type of engine, within the capacity restriction of 30 cubic centimetres. The first race under this ruling was won by Mr. G. M. Suzor, of the Paris club, with an extremely well-designed boat named *Canard*, which was fitted with a two-stroke engine of about 17 c.c., and achieved a speed of about 16 m.p.h. This race was run regularly each year up to and including 1939, and during this period speeds rose steadily up to more than 45 m.p.h., the original restriction on engine capacity remaining unaltered. The popularity of petrol-engined boats increased at a no less rapid rate of progression, and in later years it became difficult to accommodate the number of entries in the time schedule allowable for the race. Still greater popularity for the petrol engine was induced by the introduction of new racing classes for smaller engines, including the " miniature " class restricted to 15 c.c., and when organised racing is again resumed it is anticipated that it will be necessary to legislate for the classification of boats with engines down to 5 c.c. or less. The number of model speed boats fitted with petrol engines is now overwhelmingly greater than those with any other type of engine.

The writer's 15 c.c. petrol-driven hydroplane " Golly "

Mr. E. W. Vanner with an early example of a petrol-driven launch

Model Aircraft

As early as 1908, flights were made with model aeroplanes fitted with petrol engines, and in 1914 Mr. D. Stanger set up a record of 51 seconds with a model biplane propelled by a four-cylinder double-vee engine. Interest in this form of motive power was, however, very lukewarm in model aircraft circles for many years after this, and it was not until 1932 that serious attempts were made to improve on Mr. Stanger's performance. The writer claims to have been largely instrumental in bringing about a revival of interest in this field by demonstrating the possibilities of small petrol engines, and soliciting the collaboration of prominent model aircraft designers. Eventually, a model biplane, " Kanga," was built by Capt. (now Lieut.-Col.) Bowden, and fitted with an engine supplied by the writer, which put up a flight of over 70 seconds with very little effort. On the strength of this achievement, an engine was designed specially for model aircraft propulsion ;

Capt. C. E. Bowden starting his first petrol-driven model aeroplane
" Kanga "

this was fitted to a high-wing monoplane, the " Bee," which achieved a record flight on the first day out. The engine in question was known as the " Atom Minor " and had a capacity of slightly under 15 c.c. ; it will be referred to in a later chapter. Its culminating success was attained in a flight by Captain Bowden's " Blue Dragon," in which the latter rose in a tight spiral to over 4,000 ft., and was clocked " out of sight " at 12 minutes 48 seconds. As the " Blue Dragon " was later fitted with a different engine—mainly to reduce the performance, which was undesirably efficient, in view of difficulty in retrieving the plane after a long-distance run— some confusion has arisen as to the facts regarding this record flight, but it can be stated definitely that it was attained with the " Atom Minor " engine installed. Captain Bowden later employed this engine for propelling a model hydroplane, and succeeded in establishing a new record in this field also.

The " Atom Minor " may be claimed to have established beyond doubt not only the practicability, but also the fascina-

A I c.c. model aircraft engine by Mr. R. Trevithick

tion of petrol-engined model aircraft, and it was rapidly followed up by other successful engines, both in this country and abroad. It was found possible to obtain reliable and reasonably efficient performance with smaller engines, and most designers of model aircraft engines have attempted to produce engines of small capacity, but in some cases developments in this direction have been rather overdone. While it is very desirable to produce engines small and light enough to install in model aircraft of a reasonable size, the ultra-small engine often defeats its own purpose, as its weight cannot be reduced in proportion to its power output, and the power/weight ratio, therefore, becomes very poor.

One of the developments which have arisen from the widespread interest in petrol-engined model aircraft is the commercial production, in large quantities, of small petrol engines of a type suited to this and other model engineering purposes. Many types of engines, mostly of American manufacture, have been made available at prices which are within the reach of most aero-modellers. This is a great advantage to those who have not the facilities to build their own engines, but it should not be allowed to divert the attention of model engineers generally from the greater interest and pleasure to be derived from tackling the problems of engine design and construction themselves.

Racing Cars

These are comparative newcomers to the model arena, their development having been largely due to the availability of ready-made engines, and, like the latter, owing a good deal to commercial enterprise in America. In many respects racing cars resemble racing hydroplanes in their basic problems of power plant and transmission, but a car is much easier to drive at high speed than a hull, and problems of stability, although by no means non-existent, are not nearly so pronounced. The result is that it is possible to run model cars at extremely high speed with quite small engines, and the

Another view of Mr. Trevithick's 1 c.c. engine

Mr. R. H. R. Curwen's 5 c.c. model racing car

sport holds a great attraction to anyone who appreciates the thrill of speed.

As yet, model car racing has not become very firmly established in this country, but there is every reason to believe that, when more normal conditions return, its development will follow logically with the rapidly increasing popularity of model petrol engines.

Traction

Although up to the present there have been comparatively few applications of model petrol engines to this purpose, sufficient evidence exists to show that they are capable of giving quite satisfactory and reliable service in this field of duty, provided that basic problems of transmission are properly tackled. Although, from the purely utility point of view, it is possible to adapt almost any of the popular type of engines to this work, there is a very strong case for the

A group of model car racing enthusiasts at a meeting of the Pio eer Model Racing Car Club

development of a specialised type of engine in which the salient features are flexibility, wide range of control and an absence of " fussiness."

The writer has already produced one model design in which these qualities are demonstrated; namely, The Model Engineer Aveling Type DX Road Roller, which is a characteristic representation of the prototype to one-eighth scale, powered by a single-cylinder horizontal engine of 15 c.c. capacity. Many of these models have been constructed, and all have given excellent results ; this is largely due to the care taken to study the demands of both the engine and transmission gear, and to provide for them in the design.

Another venture, about which full information is not yet available, is the application of the model petrol engine to rail traction in the $3\frac{1}{2}$-in gauge model of the L.M.S. Diesel shunting locomotive " 1831." This is powered with a vertical twin engine of 30 c.c. capacity and incorporates an infinitely variable transmission gear, similar in principle to that of the road roller, but with the addition of an automatic centrifugal

An example of the " M.E." Aveling type road roller, constructed by Mr. J. Ripper

A typical example of a scale model gas engine (Photographed at the "Model Engineer" Exhibition)

clutch. Rail tests of this locomotive have not yet been carried out, but bench tests of the engine prove that the intended qualities are fully up to expectations, and little doubt is entertained as to the performance of the locomotive itself.

Stationary Engines

Models of the older types of stationary engines, which are mostly of the horizontal open type, have always been popular, and many examples of these have been running for years on both petrol and gas, in some cases being applied to practical utility purposes, such as driving electrical generators and water pumps. But recent years have seen a gradual metamorphosis of the full-sized stationary engine, which in its modern form is now usually enclosed and runs at higher speed ; the vertical cylinder arrangement is more common, and water-cooling is often replaced by forced-draught air-cooling. All these features can be reproduced in model engines, and designs are now in development which enable small-power direct-coupled generating sets to be packed into a light and compact self-contained unit, instantly available for use, and capable of running for any length of time. Some of these units have already played a part in solving war problem s and are equally suitable for any purposes where a small but continuous supply of electric power is required.

CHAPTER II

PRINCIPLES ON WHICH ENGINES WORK

IT is assumed that nearly all readers of this book will already have made it their business to become familiar with the rudimentary principles of internal combustion engines, and a lengthy discourse on this subject should not therefore be necessary in a handbook of this kind. But it is most important that these basic principles should never be lost sight of, and that there should be no misunderstanding in respect of the technical definitions which must necessarily be used from time to time in the explanation of theoretical points. It is only in this way that one can comprehend the relative advantages and limitations of various engines, and understand how particular principles or features of design affect efficiency, economy or suitability for a given form of duty. A little space is therefore devoted to discussing basic theory of motive power engine in general, and internal combustion engines in particular.

Heat Engines

All types of engines in which mechanical power is generated by the combustion of fuel are known as " heat engines "; this category includes practically all " prime movers," or actual power generators, of any size or importance used in the world to-day, with the exception of those which utilise natural forces, such as wind, falling water, or tidal energy.

In any form of heat engine, whether the fuel used is solid, liquid or gaseous, and whether it is burnt in the normal way or exploded in a closed vessel, the first principle in using it efficiently and economically is to ensure that its combustion

A 15 c.c. model aircraft engine by Mr. Gerald Smith, shown mounted upright and inverted respectively

is as perfect and complete as possible. The time factor, or, in other words, the rapidity of combustion, is also most important in some types of engines, particularly that in which we are primarily concerned in this book. The second most important principle is the efficient utilisation of the heat energy produced in the process of combustion.

Working Cycle

This term is used to define the sequence of operations employed in the process of extracting the heat energy from the fuel and turning it into mechanical power. All practical working cycles employed in heat engines are based on the " ideal heat cycle " postulated by Carnot in 1824, but, while this ideal cannot be attained in practice, the closer its conditions can be approached, the higher will be the efficiency.

Without going deeply into the theory of the Carnot cycle, it may be stated that it requires the utilisation of an infinitely wide range of temperature, through the medium of an expansible fluid such as steam, gas or air, and the complete elimination of heat losses or pressure leakage. The working cycles employed in practice fall far short of this ideal by reason of physical limitations, which will be referred to in describing them later.

Efficiency

Although the literal definition of this term is quite straightforward, it is used very loosely, even in technical circles, and the expression " high efficiency " is often used to describe an engine of high power in relation to its bulk or weight, whereas, scientifically, it means something very different. The true or " overall " efficiency of an engine depends on the actual power it produces in relation to the quantity of heat energy it consumes in fuel, but, as there are many factors in this equation, it is usual to consider them separately, under the heading " thermal efficiency," " mechanical efficiency " and " volumetric efficiency."

Thermal Efficiency

This term may be defined as the relation of the mechanical pressure energy developed in the engine cylinder to the calorific value and quantity of the fuel consumed to produce it. In practically all engines, the heat losses are relatively large, and the thermal efficiency relatively low. It is usually expressed on a percentage basis. Sometimes the term is taken to include mechanical as well as thermal losses, but this is more correctly defined as the " overall " efficiency, as mentioned above. In a general way, it may be stated that thermal losses increase as the size of the engine is reduced, so that the power actually developed by a small engine may amount to less than 10 per cent. of that theorectically obtainable, as shown by calculation of the available energy in the fuel put into it.

Mechanical Efficiency

A further loss is caused by mechanical friction in the engine itself, including that of the piston and main bearings, valve-operating mechanism, and auxiliaries, such as pumps or electrical equipment. These losses also tend to increase as the engine is reduced in size, owing to the increased ratio of friction surface in relation to volume. Small engines rarely attain more than about 80 per cent. mechanical efficiency, and may even fail to reach 50 per cent., depending partly upon mechanical complication, but also on workmanship, materials of construction, design, and lubrication.

Volumetric Efficiency

In pumps and compressors, volumetric efficiency is generally taken to mean the ratio of the fluid actually displaced, under normal working conditions and speed, to that obtained by the calculation of cylinder displacement. This definition is also applicable to engines, and is a means of assessing the power obtainable from an engine of a given size, at a given speed. But here again the term is somewhat loosely applied, being

Another model aircraft engine by Mr. Gerald Smith

often taken to mean the *total* power attainable from an engine, without taking the speed factor into account.

Volumetric efficiency is affected by restrictions in the flow of gases through valves, ports and passages, and by back pressure in the exhaust system. Small engines are, in this case also, worse situated than large ones, and increase of speed augments losses in this respect. High-speed engines are sometimes said to suffer from " poor breathing," or, in other words, loss of volumetric efficiency. Design of the essential parts which affect pumping and gas transfer is the main deciding factor.

It should be noted that volumetric efficiency has no direct effect on, or relation to, thermal and mechanical efficiency ; that is to say, it does not influence the internal economy of the engine. In calculating overall efficiency, volumetric loss is not added to or multiplied by thermal and mechanical losses, and an engine which is distinctly poor in volumetric efficiency may not only be tolerated, but may be under no practical disadvantage, for certain duties. But there are many cases where it is most important to be able to produce high power with a small engine. This is particularly evident where racing engines are classified by capacity restrictions. It is also logical to expect that a large engine will be much heavier than a small one, and thus volumetric efficiency has an important bearing on power/weight ratio, which is an essential factor in the success of engines used for propelling aircraft and similar purposes.

Internal and External Combustion Engines

Heat engines are broadly classified in two categories ; those in which the combustion and heat transfer of the fuel are effected outside the working cylinder (or other form of mechanical pressure converter) and those in which it is carried out internally. The former are apparently more simple and direct in their working principles, because the heat is simply converted into pressure through a suitable expansible medium, which is easily conveyed and controlled, so that it can be used to drive a very straightforward type of engine. Of the engines in this group, by far the most common is the steam engine, though engines have been devised to use various fluids, gases and vapours, including air, as the working medium. The principles on which such engines work need not be discussed here, as they are not within the scope of this book, and they are mentioned only by way of comparison.

Although internal combustion engines are far more complex in their functions than steam engines, they utilise a far more direct method of converting the combustion energy into mechanical pressure, and, by doing so, they eliminate many sources of heat loss in the process. Unfortunately, however, they fail to utilise the full range of temperature so effectively as the best forms of steam engines, being forced by mechanical limitations to reject the working fluid at a comparatively high temperature and pressure. But in small sizes, at least, it is generally possible in practice to make them more efficient thermally than steam engines, and an even more important consideration, in most cases, is that they can readily be made to produce considerable power in relation to their overall dimensions. This advantage often outweighs any deficiencies in respect of fuel economy, and it may be said that for any purposes where a high-power engine must be concentrated within a restricted space and weight, the small internal combustion engine is at present without a serious rival.

Four-Stroke Engines

The most common form of internal combustion engine used in full-size practice at the present day is the " four-stroke " or Otto-cycle engine, in which four complete strokes of the piston are required to complete the sequence of operations in the working cycle. These are defined as : (1) *the admission or inlet stroke*, in which the piston moves away from the closed end of the cylinder and the inlet valve opens to admit air, or a mixture of air and fuel, which is drawn into the cylinder

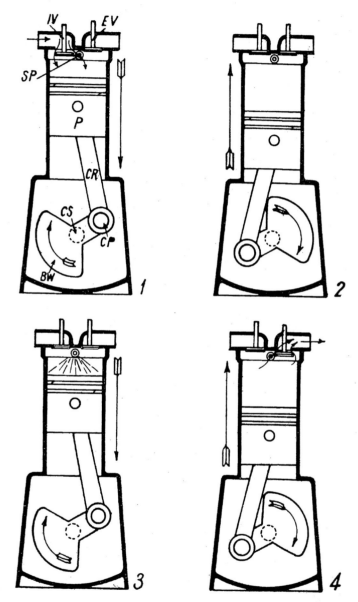

Fig. 1.—Cycle of operations in four-stroke engine

by the difference of pressure in the latter in relation to the outer atmosphere. (2) *The compression stroke*, in which the return motion of the piston compresses the air or mixture into the closed end of the cylinder, thus preparing it for rapid and efficient combustion. (3) *The firing stroke*, in which the mixture is ignited (or in some cases, fuel is injected and simultaneously ignited), thus causing an extremely rapid rise of temperature and pressure in the cylinder, by means of which mechanical effort is exerted on the piston, which again moves outwards under the effect of this force. (4) *The exhaust stroke*, in which the piston again returns, and the exhaust valve opens, so that the products of combustion are expelled from the cylinder, partly by their own pressure and partly by displacement.

This cycle of operations, which is, of course, repeated indefinitely as long as the engine runs, is fairly straightforward, and in an engine of good mechanical design and construction works reliably and produces considerable power. But in view of the fact that only one stroke in four produces power, the turning movement on the crank is intermittent, and means must be provided to sustain motion between firing strokes. This can be done by making the engine with four or more cylinders, firing at even intervals, or by providing a fairly heavy flywheel, which stores momentum during the firing stroke and releases it during the other three. In practice, a flywheel, or its equivalent, is either a necessity or an advantage in any engine, except those having a large number of cylinders.

The four-stroke engine must be equipped with valves by means of which the entry of the charge and the release of exhaust can be controlled. These are operated from the crankshaft of the engine, through reduction gearing, so that the sequence of operations is completed once in two revolutions. The most common form of valve employed for this purpose is the " mushroom," or poppet, valve, which is fairly simple to operate by means of cams, and is robust and easy to keep gastight, but almost every type of valve, including slide and rotary valves in various forms, have been used more or less successfully. Much of the functional efficiency of an engine depends on its valve gear, as opening at the wrong time, or leakage of the valve when it is closed, results in loss of pressure which should be usefully employed. The valve gear requires a certain amount of power for its operation, which must be added to frictional and other mechanical losses, but, in spite of this, a well-designed and made four-stroke engine has a higher overall efficiency than most other types of I.C. engines, and can generally be made to produce the most power in relation to its cylinder volume.

Two-Stroke Engines

In these engines, the same actual sequence of operations takes place ; that is to say, admission, compression, combustion and exhaust, but the engine is arranged to complete the cycle in two strokes instead of four. To do this, only a portion of the complete stroke can be devoted to each operation, the major portion in each case being used for compression and combustion, and the rest for exhaust and admission. As the engine is unable to make use of suction caused by the piston displacement to draw the mixture directly into the working cylinder, it is necessary to provide some sort of a charging pump for this purpose. This may take the form of a more or less normal piston displacement compressor or rotary blower, but in the great majority of small or moderate-sized engines the underside of the power piston is utilised to displace mixture in the crankcase, so that the latter acts virtually as the working chamber or cylinder of a low-pressure compressor.

The use of " crankcase compression," as it is termed, enables the construction of the engine to be kept extremely simple, though at the expense of some volumetric efficiency. Although the piston obviously displaces the same volume of air on either side in a complete stroke, and the crankcase should thus be capable of pumping sufficient mixture to fill the power cylinder, it is relatively inefficient as a compressor, because of the amount of "dead" or unswept volume inevitably present.

Another way in which simplicity is attained at the cost of efficiency is in respect of the control of exhaust and admission in the popular form of two-stroke, which is often said to be " valveless." This term is not strictly accurate, though it has no valves of the type usually employed in four-stroke engines ; the valve events are, however, controlled by ports uncovered by the piston, which thus acts as a form of slide valve. But as the motion of the piston does not correspond exactly with the timing most suitable for efficient valve operation, the engine works under an inherent disadvantage, which cannot entirely be eliminated while this method of port control is employed.

Yet another source of inefficiency in the ordinary two-stroke is the imperfect scavenging (elimination of the products of combustion from the cylinder) which results in a certain residue of exhaust gas being mixed with the fresh charge and reducing its efficiency by dilution. As the ports leading into and out of the cylinder are necessarily open at the same time, it is also possible for some of the fresh charge to escape at the exhaust port, especially if attempts are made to increase charging efficiency.

Notwithstanding these deficiencies, however, the two-stroke engine can be made to perform very satisfactorily, and, though its power output, for a given capacity, is generally lower than the four-stroke engine, and its fuel consumption higher, it is no mean rival to the latter in certain spheres. On account of its simple construction and absence of valve gearing, it can be made to show a high mechanical efficiency, and can also be very lightly built, so that its power/weight ratio is high. Up to the present, the two-stroke is the only form of engine which has been found suitable for quantity manufacture in small sizes, and it is thus the only engine normally encountered in model aircraft propulsion.

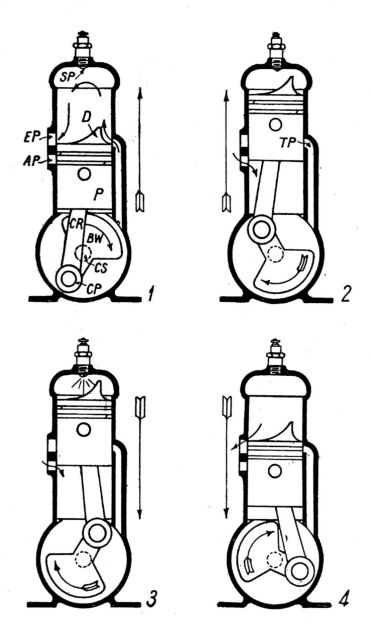

Fig. 2.—Cycle of operations in a two-stroke engine

c

Horse-Power

This is the accepted standard of performance for all engines, large and small, and may be defined simply as the rate of doing work, as measured in foot-pounds per minute. The foot-pound, which is the mechanical standard of energy, corresponding to (but not equivalent to) the watt, as used in electrical measurement, consists of the energy absorbed in raising one pound through a vertical distance of one foot. A 1 horse-power engine has the ability to perform 33,000 foot-pounds of work in one minute. It is, however, necessary to take into consideration that the term " horse-power " does not always refer to actual measurable engine power ; for instance, " N.H.P." (nominal horse-power) refers to the power of an engine as calculated from a conventional dimensional standard, as in the case of the taxation rating of a motor vehicle. " I.H.P." (indicated horse-power) is the power developed inside the cylinder of an engine, neglecting mechanical losses by the friction of its working parts. " B.H.P." (brake horse-power) is the power actually measured at the working shaft by means of an absorption brake or equivalent method, and is the only standard by which the actual performance can be assessed.

Mean Effective Pressure

In any fluid pressure engine, the force applied to the piston must necessarily vary throughout the cycle. For the purposes of calculation, it is necessary to find the average pressure, which can only be done accurately by means of elaborate equipment, not usually available for use on model engines. It is, however, usual to make more or less accurate estimates based on compression and explosion pressures, which can be used to calculate the indicated horse-power, when the dimensions and speed of the engine are also known. The formula for this calculation is the well-known $\dfrac{PLAN}{33,000}$, P representing the mean effective pressure, L the length of stroke in feet,

A the area of the piston in square inches, and N the number of working strokes per minute.

Brake mean effective pressure (" B.M.E.P.") is a purely imaginary figure, arrived at by working backwards from the known brake horse-power, as found by test, to find the value of P in the above formula. Although this is always lower than the mean effective pressure actually developed, it is an extremely useful figure to know, as it forms a basis of comparison for the performance of engines of any size and type. For instance, if we find the power of a certain engine by test, and from this calculate the B.M.E.P. as, say, 80 lb. per sq. in., we are able to apply this figure to an engine of totally different size or type to find out what its performance will be if the cylinder pressures are similar.

It should be observed that the M.E.P. of a four-stroke is usually far higher than that of a two-stroke owing to its more efficient charging. If identical pressures were obtainable in the two types of engines, it is obvious that the two-stroke would develop twice the power of the four-stroke, in engines of the same size and speed, because it has twice the number of power impulses. This ideal is eagerly pursued by many enthusiastic believers in the two-stroke engine, but, as already stated, it is uncommon for the latter type of engine even to reach equality to the four-stroke in power output; however, it is by no means certain that development of the two-stroke may not proceed eventually to bring this goal within reach.

Properties of Fuels

The power produced in any heat engine, being derived from the fuel it consumes, must obviously depend largely on the quality as well as the quantity of fuel used. Fuels of widely different quality are used in internal combustion engines, and, quite apart from the actual heat energy, or calorific value, of the fuel, there are other factors that affect the efficiency which can be obtained by its combustion, under the particular conditions which exist in an engine. All the physical properties

of the fuel have to be taken into account in this respect. It is
not proposed to give complete details of these properties here,
as they can be obtained from any standard text-book on
fuels ; but only to show their bearing on the performance of
an engine, as it is most essential that fuels should be used
intelligently to ensure the best results.

Calorific Value

This is the measure of heat value contained in a fuel, and
is expressed in British Thermal Units per pound (or gallon),
or calories per gram, of fuel. Other things being equal, the
fuel which produces the most heat will enable the utmost
power to be obtained from the engine for a given fuel consumption, so long as it does not introduce problems such as
overheating, which may cause greater waste, or mechanical
difficulties. Sometimes it is an advantage to use a fuel of lower
calorific value, if it is possible to consume it more completely
with a given quantity of air ; as, for instance, in the case of
alcohol fuel, which has a lower calorific value than petrol, but
requires less oxygen for its complete combustion. In cases
where economy of fuel is not the prime consideration, alcohol
fuel will sometimes enable greater power to be obtained from
an engine than is possible with petrol.

Flash Point

The temperature at which a fuel begins to give off an inflam-
mable vapour has an important influence on the readiness
with which it will ignite. With a fuel having a flash point
above that of the atmosphere, it may be found difficult to
start an engine unless heat is applied to the mixture or the
cylinder. Paraffin engines, for instance, often have a
" vaporiser " heated by exhaust gases, and have to be started
either by some auxiliary means of heating the vaporiser, or
by running a short time on petrol. Flash point is sometimes
confused with volatility, or the readiness with which the fuel
will vaporise or turn into a gas ; but, though these qualities

often go together, it is by no means essential for the fuel even to be partly vaporised to ensure combustion, and it may even be a disadvantage where the utmost power is required. The reason is that gas or vapour takes up much more room than " wet " spray for a given quantity of fuel, and thus leaves less space in a given cylinder volume for the oxygen required for combustion. Much the same objection applies to heating the mixture, though this may improve normal running at moderate power output.

Viscosity

This is a measure of the " stickiness " of a liquid, or its reluctance to flow through a calibrated orifice under a given pressure or gravity. Petrol has a low viscosity, and this facilitates spraying it from the carburettor jet under the influence of a comparitively low pressure. A fuel of high viscosity would need to be sprayed by means of a high-pressure pump, which is one reason why injection has always been favoured for heavy oil engines, though the modern injection engine works best on a less viscous oil than the crude oil originally employed. Specific gravity, or weight per volume, of the fuel, also affects the readiness with which it can be sprayed, but has no direct relation with viscosity. The common practice of mixing lubricating oil with the fuel in two-stroke engines increases its viscosity, and calls for a larger carburettor jet than would be necessary with plain fuel; for this reason, the same grade and proportion of oil should be maintained whenever possible, if the need for constant manipulation of jet settings is to be avoided. Viscosity varies considerably with the temperature of the fuel, and is one of the reasons why jet settings often have to be opened up to ensure easy starting from cold ; the discharge from the jet increases as the engine warms up, and allows the jet opening to be reduced.

Octane Value

Petroleum products, including petrol, are what is known as mixed hydrocarbons, containing a number of basic constituents or " fractions," all having individual properties and characteristics. Some of these " fractions," while all useful and capable of adding their quota to the power produced by combustion, may ignite less readily than others or tend to produce violent uncontrolled explosions. One of the " fractions " in petrol is known as octane, and fuel research has proved it to be one of the most valuable constituents for promoting smooth running and high power. The accepted standard of fuel quality, therefore, is taken by comparison of its behaviour in an engine, with that of pure octane. For economic reasons, it is impracticable to use fuels consisting entirely, or in major proportion, of pure octane, but it is possible, by blending fuels, or adding small proportions of chemical reagents, to modify the combustion characteristics of the fuel and thereby improve its " octane value."

High octane fuels enable engines to be run at high compression ratios without risk of " knocking " or detonation, thereby reducing mechanical wear and tear, and enabling maximum power output to be maintained. To obtain the best results from any type of engine, the fuel which is best suited to its design and characteristics should be selected and, in the pursuit of high performance, it should not be assumed that the fuel which gives the most powerful explosion is invariably the best.

CHAPTER III

VARIOUS TYPES OF MODEL PETROL ENGINES

ANYONE who has studied the design of petrol engines as used in full-size practice will realise that, quite apart from different principles of operation, there is a wide diversity in the form and arrangement of engines used for various purposes. There are several reasons for this, the most important being convenience in manufacture or installation in a particular form of machine or vehicle, and adaptation to different duties. Thus the form of engine used to propel a motor-cycle is very different from that used in aircraft, and a marine engine differs from both, although they all may work on the same principles.

This diversity exists also in the case of models, though up to the present the full range of prototype design has by no means been completely explored, and so far as commercially-produced engines are concerned, there is a tendency to exploit one type of engine to perform all sorts of different duties. But it is desirable to point out that there is no practical reason why variety in model petrol engines should be in any way restricted. It is only sound common sense to design an engine specifically to suit the job it has to perform, and while the general-purpose engine serves a very useful purpose by reason of its versatility, it should never be regarded as the one and only type of engine worth developing. In commercial production of model engines, a single engine, or a small range of types and sizes, is the most profitable policy for obvious reasons, but it is quite unnecessary and undesirable for the amateur constructor, as it engenders a monotony which detracts considerably from the interest of constructing and running engines.

Single-Cylinder Engines

The single-cylinder engine is by far the most popular in small sizes for practically all purposes, in both four-stroke and two-stroke types. It is obviously the simplest form of engine both to design and construct, but its simplicity extends much farther than this, as it applies also to adjustment, running attention, and maintenance. Until a few years ago, the single-cylinder engine was the only type which could be guaranteed to run successfully in small sizes, and many ambitious and ingenious attempts to produce model multi-cylinder engines in the past have been partial or complete failures. The position has changed somewhat now, owing to the greater amount of experience and general improvement of design, and perhaps even more by reason of the availability of reliable small accessory equipment, but even so, the beginner who attempts the construction of model petrol engines will be well advised to start off with a s i n g l e - c y l i n d e r engine.

An even greater advantage, in cases where the utmost performance of an engine of given total capacity is required, is that the single-cylinder engine has a higher mechanical efficiency than an engine having a

An experimental 30 c.c. engine by Mr. J. Latta

number of cylinders of reduced size, because of its smaller number of working parts and reduced area of rubbing surfaces in relation to capacity. Consequently, the single-cylinder engine is generally preferred for racing, and it is worthy of note that all model speed boat records of which any information is at present available have been attained with the aid of single-cylinder engines.

The majority of single-cylinder engines are of the vertical type, sometimes inverted in the case of model aircraft engines, in order to keep the centre of gravity as low as possible. (These engines will, however, usually run in any position, providing that suitable means are provided to ensure proper fuel and oil feed.) This arrangement is usually convenient for installation and accessibility, and generally favours a compact and symmetrical engine arrangement. There are, however,

certain forms of duty for which a horizontal cylinder arrangement may be preferred, as, for instance, in the conventional type of stationary engine. From the very earliest days of their development, stationary internal combustion engines have been almost

The 30 c.c. vertical twin engine for the " 1831 " locomotive, constructed by Mr. Ian Bradley universally of the horizontal type, and many very successful working models of such engines have been produced.

Twin-Cylinder Engines

When more than one cylinder is employed, the question of the relative positions of the cylinders becomes highly important. They may be placed side by side in single file, each piston working on a separate throw of the crankshaft, arranged in banks at various angles or directly opposed, or projecting radially around the crankshaft.

In the case of engines having two cylinders, there are three popular types, the " two-in-line," the " vee twin " and the " flat twin," all three of which have been modelled more or

Another view of the " 1831 " engine

less successfully. The " two-in-line " is the most straight-forward arrangement, and is readily adaptable to installation in a boat or an aeroplane. Several fairly successful two-stroke model engines of this type have been made, and a few four-strokes. The " vee twin " offers some constructional advantages in the case of the four-stroke engine, as it can be made with a single crank throw for the two cylinders, but it is by no means so well suited for construction in the form of a two-stroke, and engines of this type are rare. It is usual to make " flat " or opposed twin engines with a double crank throw, so that the pistons move always in opposite directions, and thereby assist balance. Four-stroke engines of this type fire on alternate cylinders once per revolution, but two-strokes fire simultaneously, as both pistons reach the inner end of the stroke together. Flat twin engines have been made with a single crank, so that both pistons move in the same direction ; but this destroys the self-balancing effect, and also produces

An all-fabricated 12 c.c. flat twin engine, by Mr. F. G. Arkell

Two views of a 30 c.c. four-cylinder o.h.v. engine by Mr. Elmer Wall, of Chicago

An all-fabricated side-valve water-cooled engine by Mr. F. G. Arkell

The cooling fan of Mr. Ian Bradley's 6 c.c. side-valve engine

irregular firing intervals in the case of a four-stroke engine. Two-strokes cannot be made in this way unless they are equipped with a separate charging pump, because crankcase displacement remains constant when one piston moves out as the other moves in.

The flat twin engine is often recommended for boat work, owing to its low centre of gravity and absence of vertical projections, which enable it to be installed completely below the deck line in a streamlined hull. But unless it is made with a very short stroke, its width is excessive, so that it can only be installed in a boat of very broad beam, and accessibility is liable to be difficult, even when the full width of the deck is made detachable. This type of engine has also been used for model aircraft, in which these objections do not apply, and its small frontal area is a direct advantage. There can be no doubt that it is one of the most attractive forms of design, even though its practical advantages may not be quite so real as they appear to be at first sight.

Multi-Cylinder Engines

Very few model engines, up to the present, have been made with more than two cylinders, and of those which have, the majority appear to be of the " four-in-line " type, conforming generally to the type commonly used in motor cars. It is extremely difficult to construct a successful working model multi-cylinder engine, of really small capacity and dimensions, and even more so to keep its weight down to an extent comparable with that of a single-cylinder engine of similar capacity. The four-cylinder engines so far produced have been of at least 30 c.c. capacity, and have been designed for purposes where neither bulk nor weight are tightly restricted—as, for instance, propelling a moderately fast prototype boat of the launch or cruiser type. For such a purpose they may be highly satisfactory and help to preserve scale realism, though they have no advantages over the single-cylinder from the purely utility point of view.

One or two attempts have been made to model the more complex forms of aircraft engines, such as the multi-cylinder radial, but successful examples of really small engines of this type have so far been very rare.

Cooling

The great majority of model petrol engines are air-cooled, their cylinders being simply provided with fins to present the maximum area of surface to the air. As these engines usually work under conditions where there is a fairly effective cooling draught available, this method is entirely satisfactory, providing that the design of the cooling surfaces is carefully

The fan-cooling system on one of Mr. Gerald Smith's engines

carried out, and that the engines work fairly efficiently, so that waste of heat is reduced to a minimum. If engines have to run stationary, or are enclosed so that they are not exposed to natural draught, it is possible to equip them with a fan to create the necessary flow of air, though this method has not been exploited yet in model practice to any very great extent.

Water cooling has always been popular in certain types of model engines, such as those used for stationary work or for propelling prototype boats. In stationary installations, the water is usually circulated by thermal convection from a tank of fairly large capacity in relation to the cylinder jacket, or is in some cases contained in an open hopper surmounting the latter. Boat engines have plenty of water available, and usually take water from the pond with the aid of a small rotary pump or a scoop which operates through the motion of the boat, the water being circulated through the cylinder

jacket and then discharged over the side or into the exhaust pipe. In some cases, " closed circuit " cooling, incorporating a radiator or other form of cooler, is used in boats, and is an obvious advantage where the pond water is muddy or full of vegetation.

Another fan-cooled engine by Mr. Gerald Smith

CHAPTER IV

PRINCIPLES OF FOUR-STROKE ENGINE DESIGN

OWING to the fact that the four-stroke engine produces its power by means of a single power impulse per two revolutions, it is obvious that it must be built sufficiently strongly to withstand far higher maximum stresses than those accounted for by its normal or mean loading. Taking engines of similar speed and power output, the maximum stress encountered in a four-stroke engine will be twice that of a two-stroke engine and four times that of a double-acting steam engine, though the latter cannot be truly compared with an internal combustion engine, as the pressure is applied more steadily and over a greater period of time.

One of the very first considerations in the design of any four-stroke engine, therefore, is that its structure should be strong and rigid enough to cope with heavy stresses, and that bearing surfaces should be of ample area, to enable them to be kept lubricated and to withstand wear. It is possible to increase the number of power impulses, and therefore to reduce the rates of maximum to mean stress by dividing the power between a number of cylinders, but for reasons already discussed, this is not usually desirable in small engines, and in any case the stresses in individual cylinders are bound to be fairly high. It is only in very large engines that anything can be saved in respect of structural bulk or weight by using more than one cylinder, and in engines of sizes within the scope of this book the balance is more likely to be on the other side.

While flimsy construction of four-stroke engines must at all costs be avoided, however, it is a mistake to suppose that sheer massiveness, as such, can be regarded as a cardinal virtue. In engines where bulk and weight are no objection, heavy structural sections may help to absorb shocks and promote steady running, but there are many cases where the entire object of the engine may be defeated by indulging in these somewhat primitive methods. Engines can be built lightly and still kept adequately strong by disposing the design of the main components so that they offer direct resistance to the stresses imposed on them. Although this is quite a logical, and indeed obvious, basic principle of design, it is surprising how often it is forgotten or, at any rate, disregarded. Conventional forms of design are generally sound in principle, and have stood the test of time, but it would be idle to deny that they have their limitations, or that they may possibly fail to cope with new and different conditions, in engines of increasing performance and reduced weight.

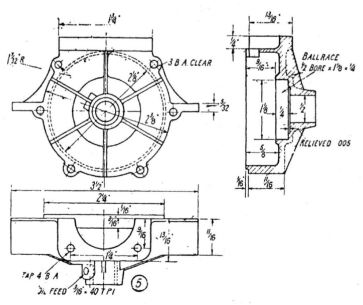

Fig. 3.—Crankcase of " Kittiwake " 15 c.c. engine (front half)

Crankcase Design

The crankcase is a very important structural component in nearly all petrol engines, as it is called upon to resist the torque of the main shaft and also the tensional stress tending to force the cylinder and the shaft apart. Most model petrol engines have the crankcase designed on somewhat similar principles to that of the conventional motor-cycle engine, which has evolved from that employed on the early Daimler and De Dion engines. That is to say, it consists of two shallow and more or less symmetrical cups, with concentric bearing housings in their endplates, and joined together at the edges by a number of bolts around the circumference. This type of crankcase is fairly easy to produce in such a way as to ensure correct alignment of the main bearings, and may be very

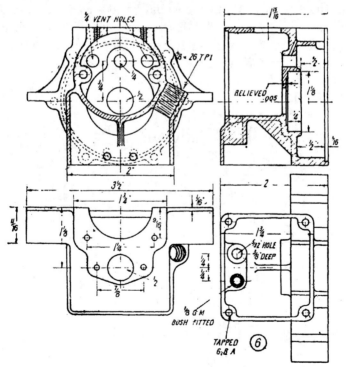

Fig. 4.—" Kittiwake " crankcase (rear half)

lightly built, providing that ribs or struts are provided to reinforce the heavily-stressed portions, such as the bearing housings. The multiplicity of bolts used to join the halves may be considerably reduced in a small engine, six or even four being adequate in many cases.

Modifications of this form of crankcase include the barrel type, with endplates on one or both sides to carry the bearings and to enable the crank to be assembled. A variant of the vertically-jointed crankcase is that having a horizontal division, which splits the main bearing housings. This is less common in single than in multi-cylinder engines, and is not quite so simple in form, but it can be designed so as to provide exceptional rigidity for very low weight.

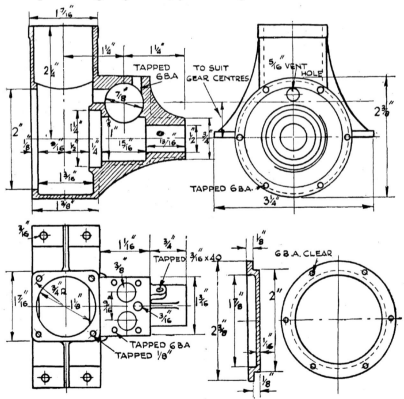

Fig. 5.—Crankcase and end cover of " Apex Minor " engine

Open-crank petrol engines are rarely made in any size nowadays and, with the exception of the horizontal stationary type, have never been popular as models. Nevertheless, there is something to be said for an engine with visible crank motion, in cases where extremely high rotational speed is not required, and models of the older types of open marine I.C. engines would be extremely interesting to construct, and quite suitable for use in prototype power boats.

In common with most other structural components, crank-cases are usually made from castings, the material most suitable for all engines, except those in which weight is unlimited, being aluminium or other light alloys. Iron is often used for structural castings of stationary engines, and brass or gunmetal has occasionally been preferred for marine engines, to avoid the corrosion which sometimes occurs when light alloys come in contact with water. Brass or steel sheet-metal crankcases, fabricated by brazing or welding, have been used successfully in a few cases, but this form of construction tends to restrict the scope of design or, at least, to favour severe and simple shapes, which are not always the most efficient. Examples of crankcases machined from solid metal, -nostly light alloy, are sometimes encountered.

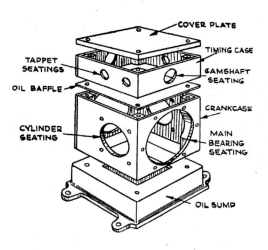

The fabricated crankcase of Mr. F. G. Arkell's flat twin engine

Cylinders

The cylinder barrel of a four-stroke engine is usually of simple design, being little more than a plain tube with provision for attachment to the crankcase and equipped with radiating fins or a water jacket for cooling. In the case of side-valve engines, which are not, however, very popular as models, valve pockets may be provided in the cylinder casting ; but overhead-valve engines usually have the valve pockets in an entirely separate combustion head casting. The material most suitable for cylinders, from the point of view of wear, is close-grained cast iron, but the low tensile strength of this material is a disadvantage when light construction is essential. Steel cylinders, turned inside and out to very thin section, have been suc-

cessfully used for light-weight engines, but it should be observed that too thin a cylinder barrel is undesirable, as it retards the conduction of heat and is liable to distortion, to say nothing of the risk of accidental damage. Light construction, combined with good heat conductivity, is sometimes obtained by using a light alloy barrel with an inserted thin steel or cast-iron liner.

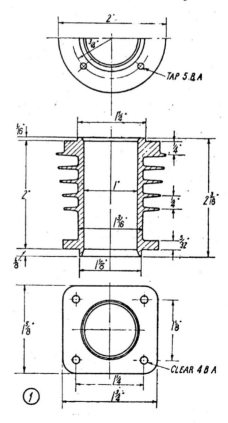

Cylinder of " Kittiwake "
engine

A flange is usually provided near the base of the cylinder for attaching the latter to the crankcase by four or more studs, but an alternative method is to employ long studs which extend past the cylinder barrel and bear on or in the cylinder head. As these hold the barrel in compression, it is sometimes claimed that they overcome the handicap of low tensile strength in a light cast-iron cylinder ; but they often introduce disadvantages by elongation under stress, or by variable heat expansion, and are not so popular now as formerly. The use of this method of attachment should not be an excuse for eliminating the cylinder base flange entirely, as the latter has an important steadying influence and helps to maintain the cylinder exactly square with the main bearings, a most essential condition for mechanical efficiency.

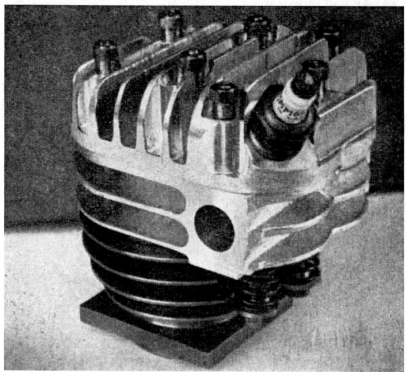

The cylinder of Mr. Ian Bradley's 6 c.c. side-valve engine

A 15 c.c. o.h.v. engine by Mr. Elmer Wall

The utmost care should be taken in boring and finishing the cylinder to ensure accuracy and thereby enable the piston and rings to fit properly and retain compression. Small engines will often refuse to run at all if there is a leakage of gas past the piston and, even if they do run reasonably well under such conditions, it is obvious that there must be a serious loss of efficiency through the loss of the charge before ignition, and of working pressure after ignition. But in addition, leakage of burning gas will cause the piston to overheat, and may lead to mechanical trouble by destroying the oil film on the cylinder walls.

Cylinder Heads

In the orthodox form of overhead-valve engine, the valves are usually arranged either parallel to each other and in line with the cylinder axis or inclined at an angle on either side of the latter. Modern practice in high-efficiency engines favours inclined valves, as it is possible to accommodate larger valves in relation to the size of the cylinder and to employ an efficiently-shaped combustion chamber, besides which the spreading-out of the valves enables the head to be better cooled externally. The parallel valve arrangement tends to restrict the size of valve ports which can be used and to cramp the valve-operating gear, but it is simpler to produce, especially in respect of machining problems, and enables the simplest and most efficient form of valve operating rocker gear to be employed. Where extremely high compression ratios are considered desirable, it is often difficult to use inclined valves, even when the crown of the piston is elaborately shaped to clear them.

Up to the present, there is no definite evidence to show which form of valve arrangement produces the highest ultimate efficiency, and it has been shown, both by racing results and brake tests, that engines can be made to attain extremely high performance with either.

The employment of side valves involves the use of an

elongated combustion chamber and restricts the compression ratio which can be usefully employed, but careful design of the head enables these disadvantages to be reduced to a minimum. On the other hand, side valves reduce the complication of the valve gear, improve its mechanical efficiency and promote smooth and silent operation ; they also enable the overall height of the engine and, to some extent, its weight, to be reduced.

Crankshafts

The crankshaft is the most heavily-stressed working component in the engine, and should be sufficiently sturdy in design to resist measurable deflection under load. A " full " crankshaft, that is to say, one supported by main bearings on both sides of the crankpin, is usually employed on a four-stroke engine, as this is convenient to enable the timing gear to be

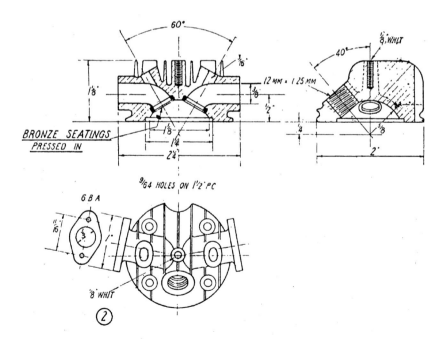

Fig. 8.—Cylinder head of " Kittiwake " engine

driven from one end of the crankshaft and the flywheel to be mounted on the other. The overhung type of crankshaft is not very popular on this type of engine, though it may be used in conjunction with a " follower " or driver crank, or with certain modified arrangements of timing gear. If properly designed and housed in rigid bearings, the overhung crank is quite satisfactory, and may in some cases be less prone to deflection than the usual type of full crankshaft.

Crankshafts may be made in one piece, either by cutting from solid bar or forging to shape prior to machining, or may be fabricated by various methods, including brazing and welding. Built-up shafts, which can be dismantled and re-assembled, are rather difficult to accommodate in small engines where bulk and weight are restricted, but have been successfully employed in many cases ; if properly designed and accurately constructed, they are capable of being used for very heavy duty. This type of crankshaft, in common with the overhung crank, enables the connecting-rod to be made with a solid eye at the big end, thereby reducing complication and risk of mechanical trouble.

The form of crankshaft commonly employed on motor-cycle engines, having the webs extended into discs of large diameter to form internal flywheels, is equally applicable to models, but has certain practical disadvantages in many cases, and it requires a crankcase of extra large diameter, which may be

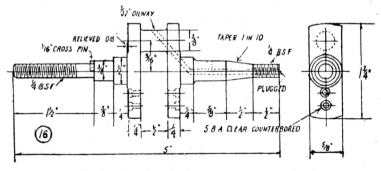

Fig. 9.—Crankshaft of " Kittiwake " engine

Crankcase components of Wall 15 c.c. o.h.v. engine

Crankshaft, connecting rod, and piston assembly of Wall "Mariner" 30 c.c. twin two-stroke

difficult to accommodate in restricted space and also tend to increase the weight of the engine.

Crankshafts may be run in plain bearings or fitted with ball or roller races on the main journals, and sometimes the crankpins as well. Plain bearings have the advantage of simplicity and minimum weight, and are perfectly satisfactory in most cases, but for very high duty it is desirable to use hardened journals, in order to promote durability and reduce friction. Standard ball or roller races can be fitted to unhardened shafts, and it is probable that this constitutes their main practical advantage, as in other respects they work under rather unfavourable conditions and do not realise the theoretical ideal of eliminating friction by true rolling action. The large diameter and weight of standard races is often inconvenient, but construction of crankshafts with hardened journals, to run in direct contact with the balls or rollers, is difficult and, indeed, hardly practicable with ordinary equipment. This applies equally to the use of such bearings on the crankpin ; in one or two cases, standard ball races have been successfully used here, but generally a plain bearing is found more satisfactory.

Connecting Rods

It is desirable to keep the weight of the connecting rod as low as possible in high speed engines, and therefore the usual practice is to employ light I-beam section or tubular rods to sustain heavy load without deflection. Duralumin or other high-tensile light alloys are often used in preference to steel, and in nearly all cases the rods are machined from the solid, though there one or two successful examples of fabricated rods in existence.

The split big-end bearing is employed extensively in model engines, but is extremly difficult to design and fit so as to ensure an ample margin of strength without introducing excessive bulk and weight. At the best, it may be said that there is always an element of risk in the use of a split big-end in engines intended for very high speed and performance. To reduce this as far as possible, the utmost care must be taken in fitting the halves of the bearing together, and high-tensile bolts fitted, with keeps to prevent them from slackening.

Duralumin rods may be used with unbushed big and little end bearings, if the crank and gudgeon pins are hardened and highly polished and lubrication is ample, but steel rods require bushing at both ends. Unless weight is of the utmost importance, it is always a good policy to bush the eyes of the rods to enable the bearings to be renewed when worn. For engines of moderate performance, cast-bronze connecting rods give very satisfactory service and require no bushes, but they are

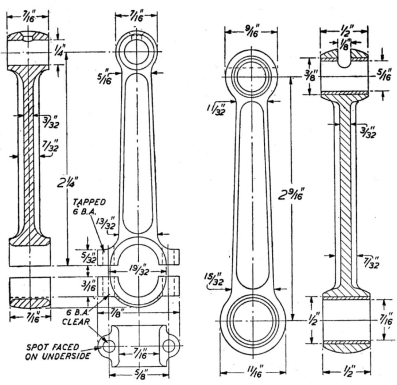

Fig. 10.—Split connecting rod   Fig. 11.—Solid connecting rod

heavier and a good deal less strong than either steel or duralumin rods, and are not recommended for very high duty.

Pistons

These again must be reduced in weight as much as possible, as they constitute reciprocating weight which can never be balanced out completely. Even in a slow-speed engine, a heavy piston is a disadvantage, and in high-performance engines the weight of the piston may be a serious limiting factor in speed and power output. Light alloy pistons are almost universally used in the latter case, but it is most important that the alloy employed should be one which has been proved suitable for this purpose. Ordinary aluminium alloys have not the necessary wearing properties for use as pistons, and their high coefficient of expansion creates difficulties in fitting them so as to withstand high temperature and at the same time avoid undue slackness when cold. The really important advantage of light alloy pistons is their superior heat conductivity, which simplifies the problem of piston cooling in highly-stressed engines.

Cast-iron pistons can be fitted to much closer clearances than those of light alloy, and generally run with less friction. In many small engines, they give far more satisfactory results than light alloy pistons, and it is possible to machine them to a very thin section, so that their weight is not excessive. Fabricated steel pistons have been used successfully in some cases, usually consisting of a very light shell, with gudgeon-pin bosses brazed or welded in.

In order to combine the advantages of steel or cast-iron pistons with the better heat conductivity of light alloy, composite construction has been employed to good effect, the crown of the piston being made of light alloy and the skirt of the harder metal. Provided that the parts can be joined in such a way as to avoid risk of loosening or detachment in service, or gas leakage at the joint, this form of piston has much to commend it, but it is no easy problem to ensure these advantages and at the same time keep the weight as low as that of the best forms of one-piece pistons.

Many small engines have no piston rings fitted and, provided the initial accuracy of both cylinder and piston is good enough and the material of both selected for durability in

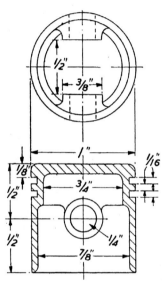

service, they give fairly satisfactory results over a moderate period of wear—probably long enough to satisfy most users of such engines. Lubrication plays an important part in maintaining efficiency in such cases, and must be adequate, as the oil film on the piston is much more easily broken down than when rings are fitted. In engines of anything larger than about ¾-in. bore, it has been found that properly-fitted rings produce an improvement, not only in the efficient working life of the engine, but also in its performance and general behaviour. Contrary to common opinion, the fitting of accurate and correctly-proportioned rings does not measurably increase piston friction. It is not usual to fit more than two rings, and refinements such as special oil-control rings are rarely found worth while in engines of the sizes dealt with in this book.

Fig. 12—Piston for " Kiwi " engine

Valve-Operating Gear

The most popular method of operating the valves of model four-stroke engines is by means of push rods and overhead rockers from cams and tappets of normal design. Although many engines have been fitted with overhead camshafts and other forms of valve mechanism, there is no reason to believe

E

that any practical advantages have ever been attained by such methods, and where the aim is high performance, the most simple and direct means of operation generally give the best results. It should be remembered that mechanical efficiency is a most important factor in the success of small engines, and that it is liable to be lowered very seriously by complicated mechanism or extra gearing. There is, however, a great deal of scope for good design in the layout of the simpler forms of operating gear, and pains taken in this respect are well repaid by durable and efficient performance.

In engines having vertical or, more correctly speaking, parallel valves, the overhead rocker is simply a plain beam pivoted in the centre, with means of engagement with the push rod at one end and a finger to engage the valve at the other. Inclined valves call for an offset rocker, with the two arms disposed at a suitable angle to work as near as possible to a right angle to the valve and push rod respectively. In all cases the rocker and push rod assembly should be laid out, by the application of simple geometry, in such a way that the

Vertical overhead valve gear of " Kiwi " engine

minimum side stresses are imposed on the valves and push rods in the course of operation. The use of side valves will, of course, eliminate the need for any push rod or rocker gear, and enable the valves to be located in line with the cams and tappets, so as to be operated from them directly.

Timing Gear

The most common method of driving the cams at half engine speed is by spur gearing from the crankshaft and, assuming that the gears are of good quality and properly meshed, this is probably the most efficient form of gearing. Bevel gearing is generally used for overhead camshaft drive, but it is more difficult to produce in an efficient form than spur gearing and requires very close mesh adjustment. Skew gearing is used extensively for driving the side camshaft used on horizontal stationary engines, and is also applied to some types of vertical engines as a means of facilitating compact layout and direct valve operation. This form of gearing involves fairly heavy end thrusts on both shafts, but so long as due

Inclined overhead valve gear of "Kittiwake" engine (rocker box cover removed)

provision is made to deal with the bearing loads thus produced, this does not necessarily result in mechanical trouble or
inefficiency. In all cases, it is desirable to use the least number
of gears which will produce the required result, because each
stage of gearing involves some loss by mechanical friction,
however well it is designed and produced.

Cams

The rules for the design of valve-operating cams are the
same as those for full-sized engines, and space does not allow
of pursuing this topic in great detail. In engines of moderate
performance, quite simple cams will produce very good
results, but when designing engines for racing purposes, very
close study of the cam design is necessary to obtain the most
efficient results at high r.p.m. Incorrect cams not only limit
performance, but may also impose abnormal loads on the
valves and the entire timing gear, sometimes causing breakages
of valves, springs and gear teeth, and always causing rapid
wear of these parts, the camshaft bearings and the cams
themselves.

Briefly, it may be stated that there are three types of cams
used for operating I.C. engine valves, namely the " tangential " cam, the " convex-flank " cam and the " constant-
acceleration " cam. The tangential cam is the simplest type,
and, as its name implies, has flanks which form a tangent to
the base circle, the nose being rounded off. This form of cam
works most efficiently with a rounded or " roller " follower.
Cams having convex flanks are the most popular in present-day
practice, as they are easily produced by manufacturing
methods and work efficiently in conjunction with flat-faced
followers or " mushroom " tappets. It is possible to design
cams of this type so that they produce results almost as good
as the " constant acceleration " cam, the shape of which is
arrived at mathematically to produce the most efficient
motion of the valve possible.

The design of cams must always be considered in conjunction

with, and relation to, that of the " followers " or tappets with which they engage. Followers of special shape, or having motion other than in a straight line, complicate cam design, and, for this reason, plain tappets operating direct on the cams are preferable to pivoted cam rockers on the grounds of straightforward design. Carefully-designed cams very much ease the loads on the tappets, push rods, rockers and valves, and enable high speeds to be obtained without excessively strong valve springs. Valve bounce, which is often very troublesome on high-speed engines, should be tackled, not by abnormally increasing the strength of valve springs, but by careful investigation of cam design and the reduction of unnecessary inertia in all working parts of the operating gear.

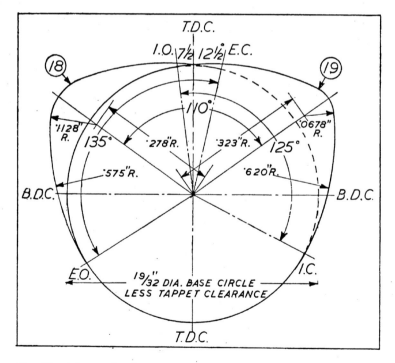

Fig. 13.—Inlet and exhaust cams for "Kittiwake" engine (designed by Mr. D. H. Chaddock)

Valves

These again may be designed by reference to full-sized
practice, the conditions being somewhat less exacting in the
case of model engines and, as the latter do not usually run for
very long periods, the use of special heat-resisting steels is not
so imperatively necessary. A medium nickel-chrome constructional steel has been found to give good results in model
engines of high performance, and in less highly-stressed
engines, valves of mild or low alloy steel have been found
entirely satisfactory.

The advantages of double or triple valve springs are not so
pronounced as in full-sized engines, but in some cases low-
inertia springs (such as " hairpin " springs) have been applied
to good effect. Special spring steel to withstand high temperature should not be necessary in model engines with
reasonably efficient cooling.

One of the difficulties in very small valves is to provide a
secure and robust means of retaining the spring. Owing to the
small size of the valve stem, cotters or pins which necessitate
drilling the stem are only permissible in cases where the
stresses are comparatively low. In high performance engines,
the horseshoe collar engaging a groove in the valve stem, as
shown in the photograph on page 86, may be used, but
a better method of spring retention is shown in Fig. 14
and consists of a soft-steel wire ring which is clenched
into a groove in the valve stem with a pair of pliers
and retained by a close-fitting counterbore in the spring
collar. Another method extensively used in full-size

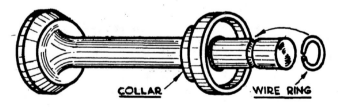

COLLAR   WIRE RING

Fig. 14.—How the valve spring collar of the " Kiwi " engine is retained

practice is the split collet retainer, as employed in the " Kittiwake " engine, and shown in Fig. 15. Screwed valve collars have been successfully used on some small engines and, so long as efficient means of locking them can be provided, there is no objection to their use. It is possible to use the screwed collar as a means of tappet adjustment, and this is done in the case of the 5-c.c. "Kinglet" engine. In this case, accidental slackening off of the spring collar locking nut simply results in raising the valve off its seating and stopping the engine, but usually the effect of the spring retaining device failing in its function is disastrous.

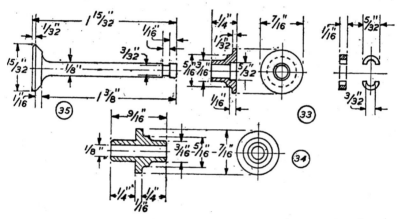

Fig. 15.—Complete valve assembly (less spring) for " Kittiwake " engine

CHAPTER V

PRINCIPLES OF TWO-STROKE ENGINE DESIGN

In respect of constructional design, much of the advice which has been given regarding the four-stroke engine applies to a greater or less extent in the case of the two-stroke. As already explained, the lower mechanical stresses encountered in the latter enable it to be built lighter practically everywhere, but sound mechanical principles should never be disregarded, and it is just as important to design essential structural parts so as to make the utmost effective use of every bit of metal in engines where power/weight ratio is important.

Crankcase Design

In normal types of two-stroke engines complete enclosure of the crankcase is a vital necessity, as it forms a pump chamber, and its internal volume must be reduced to the minimum, compatible with allowing sufficient space for the working parts, in order to eliminate unnecessary "dead space," which reduces the pressure obtainable in the crankcase, and thus lowers its efficiency as a charging pump. The higher the speed at which an engine is intended to run, the greater is the pressure required to force the mixture into the cylinder in the short period when the charging or "transfer" port is open. Many high-performance two-stroke engines have been fitted with filling pieces inside the crankcase to ensure the very minimum possible clearance everywhere, but these measures are liable to defeat their own purpose if they obstruct the free flow of the mixture into or out of the crankcase. As a general rule, it may be stated that it is better to study the most efficient design of ports and passages, with a view to obtaining the easy and most rapid flow of the mixture, than to adopt extreme measures for raising the crankcase pressure. High charging efficiency is of no practical benefit if it is cancelled out by low mechanical efficiency caused as a result of excessive pumping load.

The form of crankcase most popular in four-stroke engine practice, having the division on the vertical centre line, with a main bearing in each half and the cylinder seating on a flat platform on its top surface, is fully practicable for two-stroke engines also, and is by no means uncommon, but more or less extensive modifications to it are the rule rather than the exception. Simplicity of design in all its practical aspects is generally exploited to the utmost in these engines, and as the majority of them have " overhung " or single-bearing crankshafts, it becomes possible to make the crankcase in one piece, except for a simple cover or endplate to afford facility for internal assembly. A variation of this principle consists of making the crankcase with a plain blank end and fitting the main bearing housing in a flanged endplate ; this method may assist in solving assembly problems in some cases.

The combination of the crankcase with the cylinder (or its outer integument) in a single casting is fairly common in model two-stroke engine design. There is more in this than mere simplification of structure or reduction in the number of parts ; it can be exploited as a means of reducing the weight of the engine very substantially, with no reduction of structural strength, and also to facilitate the casting-in of passages and port faces. A very successful application of this form of design may be found in the 15-c.c. "Atom Minor" engine, in which the cylinder, with its cooling fins, transfer passage, and exhaust and inlet port faces, are integrally combined with the crankcase barrel, the two ends of which are open and provided with means of attaching the main bearing housing one side and a blank endplate on the other.

A modification of this form of design consists of carrying the crankcase up to about half the height of the cylinder and casting in the passages and port faces as before ; the finned portion of the cylinder is, however, integral with its liner and projects from the top of the crankcase. This has been adopted in the original " Atom " engine, the 6-c.c. " Atom Minor " engine, and the 5-c.c. " Kestrel " engine. In the latter, the crankcase is integral with the main bearing housing, but the original " Atom " engine has a detachable housing, and in the 6-c.c. "Atom Minor" both the housing and the blank endplate are detachable.

Cylinders

The cylinder barrel of the orthodox two-stroke engine is more complex than its counterpart in the four-stroke engine, as it must be equipped with ports and passages. If the cylinder

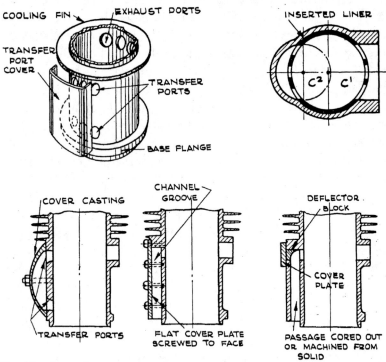

Fig. 16.—Examples of cylinder construction for model two-stroke engines

is made in one piece, either by casting, fabrication or machining, it is liable either to be heavy or to involve a good deal of work. The fitting of a sleeve or liner to an outer cast barrel or jacket will often enable both design and construction to be simplified in engines of small capacity, and so long as it is accurately machined and fitted to close limits, so as to ensure efficient heat conductivity and prevent leakage between the liner and jacket, is perfectly satisfactory in use. In order to keep weight down as low as possible, it is usual to make the outer jacket of light alloy and fit a liner of as thin a section as practicable, made of steel or cast iron. In spite of the difference in the coefficient of expansion of the metals used for the two respective parts, slackening of the liner at high temperatures is rarely experienced, mainly because the latter is always hotter than the jacket, and any tendency for the clearance between them to increase would accentuate the difference of temperature by reducing the efficiency of the heat conduction.

In the case of water-cooled engines, the water may be circulated between the outer barrel and the liner, thus ensuring the maximum cooling efficiency and at the same time simplifying casting and constructional problems. This form of construction is defined as the " wet liner " system, to distinguish it from the " dry liner " system, in which the jacket embodies a continuous inner sleeve which fits closely around the liner throughout its full length so that the latter does not make direct contact with the cooling water. Both methods have their advantages and limitations, but for small engines the wet liner is considered preferable — always subject,

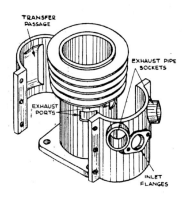

TRANSFER PASSAGE

EXHAUST PIPE SOCKETS

EXHAUST PORTS

INLET FLANGES

Fig. 17.—A method of constructing the cylinder of high - performance engines

however, to the observance of sound design and accurate workmanship in its execution.

The usual method of fitting the liner to its jacket is by shrinking in, a method which calls for machining of both parts to accurate limits and results in a permanent assembly, which cannot be dismantled without at least some risk of damage or complete destruction of one or other of the two components. A moderately tight press-fit is, however, satisfactory in engines of small capacity, and the design may be arranged so that the liner is capable of removal. Wherever possible, a rim or other locating surface should be provided on the liner, so that its endwise position may be definitely fixed, and no risk of its shifting under any circumstances can exist. Tight contact of the jacket and liner are essential in the region of gas ports, water joints, or where heat conduction takes place, but there is no necessity for it in other parts, and the fit may be made easier or definitely relieved with advantage in respect of the force required in fitting or removing the liner.

In small air-cooled engines, the fitting of a jacket around the finned portion of the cylinder rarely shows any saving in weight, and where the cylinder capacity is less than about 6 or 7-c.c., the balance is generally the other way round. It is often better in such cases to make the

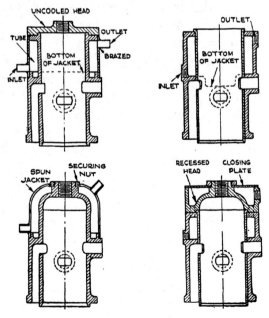

Fig. 18.—Some examples of water-cooled cylinders

cooling fins integral with the liner, and jacket only the lower portion up to the level of the top of the exhaust port face. The liner or, as it may be termed, the cylinder proper, may readily be machined from the solid, and its weight kept down to the minimum. This method of construction is adopted on the "Atom I," "Atom Minor" 6-c.c., and "Kestrel" engines.

Apart from other constructional advantages, machining the cylinder or liner all over tends to reduce the risk of distortion, which is always present when an irregularly-shaped cylinder is unevenly heated. The aluminium jacket, having better heat conductivity than the liner, distributes the temperature more equally, and even if it should distort slightly, is unlikely to force the liner out of true cylindrical shape.

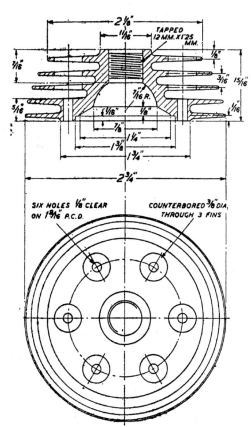

Cooling fins, whether cast or machined, should always be tapered and provided with a fillet at the root to ensure the maximum conducting efficiency. Parallel grooves, with sharp internal corners, may actually retard heat conduction from the cylinder instead of promoting it. Generally,

Fig. 19.—Cylinder head of "Atom V" 30 c.c. engine

there is very little difficulty in keeping small cylinders cool, unless the thermal efficiency of the engine is very poor, resulting in excessive waste of heat; but racing engines demand good cooling efficiency, and the design and arrangement of the finning may be important. It is a mistake to assume that this object is best served simply by crowding on closely-spaced fins, or making them abnormally deep, to provide the maximum projected surface area ; moderate spacing and depth of fins generally produce the best results.

Cylinder Heads

In contrast to the cylinder head of a four-stroke engine, that of a two-stroke is essentially little more than a mere cover or closure to seal the end of the cylinder and carry the sparking plug. This does not mean, however, that there is no scope for good design in it, or that it has no effect on engine efficiency. On the other hand, it can be shown that cylinder-head design is a very important factor in high performance, and a fruitful field for advanced research. In engines of moderate performance, however, the most important point is to arrange for adequate cooling of the head and the avoidance of distortion at high temperature, also to shape it internally so as to promote efficient combustion with the minimum heat loss. It should always be remembered that, as the actual combustion takes place in the head, there is much more heat transmitted to it than to the cylinder barrel ; consequently, it should be the first thing to be considered where cooling problems are concerned.

Water-cooled engines should, wherever possible, be provided with jacket space right over the head, particularly in the region of the sparking plug, but care must be taken to arrange the water passages so that no trapping of water or steam can take place. Air-cooled engines should have the head at least as well provided with fins as the barrel. There are several alternative methods of arranging the fins on the head, all of them capable of giving good results if properly carried out.

A simple method of producing the fins, when the cylinder is machined from the solid, is to turn them as horizontal and concentric rings, and apart from the matter of appearance, this enables an adequate cooling surface to be provided, and is entirely satisfactory in engines of the highest performance.

Sharp internal corners should never be allowed inside the combustion space, as they needlessly increase the area of surface exposed to flame temperature, and are difficult to scavenge properly ; it is possible for burning gases to be left in a corner, especially when carbon is present, sufficiently long to cause pre-ignition on the next compression stroke. A hemispherical or " domed " head is best from the point of view of thermal efficiency, but is at a disadvantage when it is necessary or desirable to use a high compression ratio, in which case an oblate or flattened head, with well-rounded corners, is preferable. Even this, however, does not allow of very high compression ratios in engines having a piston deflector of more or less normal design, and it becomes necessary to shape the inside of the head to conform to some extent with the contour of the piston crown. From this point onwards, combustion head design tends to become somewhat

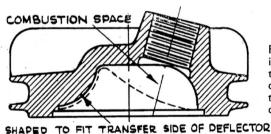

COMBUSTION SPACE

SHAPED TO FIT TRANSFER SIDE OF DEFLECTOR

Fig. 20.— Diagrams illustrating characteristics of various cylinder heads. Piston at t.d.c. indicated by dotted line

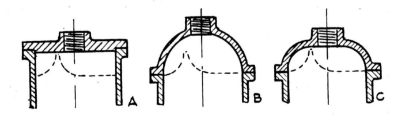

A B C

complicated, and effciency depends very largely on the proper co-relation between the shape of the head in relation to the piston, the port design, and the position of the sparking plug.

High turbulence of the gases in the cylinder immediately prior to ignition is always conducive to combustion efficiency, but it is important that this should not interfere with gas flow during the scavenging period, a condition not always easy to ensure in practice. A very successful form of combustion head, which gives good results in engines having a compression ratio of 8 or 9 to 1, is that in which the interior contour is made to conform fairly closely to that of the piston on the transfer side of the deflector only ; the best position for the plug is at an angle, on the exhaust port side, though the vertical, central position also gives good results. This form of head was very successfully employed in " Atom III." Filling pieces inside the head should always be cast or machined integral with it ; if made separately and attached by screws or rivets, the heat transmission may be faulty and allow them to become incandescent, and there is also a risk of their becoming detached, with disastrous results. Properly ordered turbulence in the cylinder not only promotes combustion efficiency, but also assists in avoiding local overheating of both the head and the piston.

There has lately been some debate as to whether cylinder heads should be made integral with the cylinder, or detachable. Whatever may be the pros and cons of the two methods, from the point of view of commercial production or utility, the detachable head has overwhelming advantages for amateur-built and experimental engines, as it not only facilitates accurate finishing and gauging of the cylinder bore but also enables compression to be altered, and other modifications made with the minimum trouble.

Pistons

The close contact of the piston, throughout its entire length with the cylinder wall, is most important in a two-stroke, as it is required to act as a valve to control the cylinder ports. Clearances must, therefore, be kept as fine as possible, and all precautions taken to avoid excessive wear, which is bound to affect efficiency far more than in the case of the four-stroke. This is particularly important in the smaller sizes of engines, in which piston rings are often dispensed with and the piston simply fitted to the closest possible working clearance. Packing grooves, to assist in maintaining an oil seal, are not permissible in two-stroke engines, or at any rate must not pass completely round the piston, as they would form leakage paths between the exhaust and transfer ports. The piston must always be slightly longer than its own stroke, to avoid uncovering the ports at both ends of its travel.

As already discussed in connection with four-stroke engines, lightness of the piston is extremely desirable to reduce unbalanced weight, but the larger clearances necessary with light alloy pistons generally result in some loss of port sealing efficiency. It can be said without hesitation that cast-iron pistons are preferable in the latter respect and are almost a necessity when no rings are fitted. To cope with the requirements of heat conductivity, there is a strong case for the use of composite pistons, which have been successfully used on several experimental engines by the writer.

Deflector Design

The early types of two-stroke engines had rather primitive types of deflectors, consisting of nothing more than a thin vertical baffle cast on the crown of the piston. This served its purpose fairly well, except that it failed to conduct heat away sufficiently rapidly for heavy duty, and thus became overheated. A thicker deflector, heavily filleted at the root, is better in the latter respect, but increases the weight of the piston more than is desirable. To remedy this, the deflector is (in full-sized engines) cast hollow, and its shape is dictated by the requirements of scavenging, cooling and compression ratio, an attempt being made to compromise between the

F

incompatibilities of the three factors. Sometimes the deflector is so designed that it can be machined, a very desirable provision to ensure uniformity of results.

The height of the deflector is also a compromise in most cases ; a high deflector is desirable for good scavenging, but makes balancing and cooling more difficult and prevents a high compression ratio from being obtained. As a general rule, it is not desirable to reduce the height of the deflector to less than the depth of the exhaust port ; preferably, it should be a little higher. Its shape, in plan view, is capable of a good deal of variation to suit the disposition of the ports, but a straight deflector gives good results and, in the smaller engines, at any rate, the simpler the better. The sides of the deflector should always be relieved, so that they do not touch the cylinder walls.

By the complete elimination of the piston deflector, in the so-called " flat top " engine, all these deflector problems are removed in one stroke, but those of port design tend to become accentuated. The cleaner design of the piston simplifies both cooling and balancing, while the design of the cylinder head is also simplified, and it is probable that much of the practical benefit of this type of engine is derived from the improvement in the shape of the combustion chamber. It is open to debate

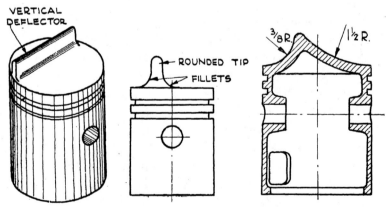

Fig. 21.—Different types of piston deflectors

or, at any rate, to the test of practical experience, whether these advantages are so pronounced in small engines as they are in larger ones and, following a good deal of experimental work, the writer is inclined to favour a form of piston design which aims at a compromise between the two types. That is to say, the use of a modified deflector of symmetrical shape, in conjunction with ports which follow the principles commonly employed in " flat-top " engines. An example of this policy is to be found in " Atom V."

Port Design

This is the most difficult problem in two-stroke engine

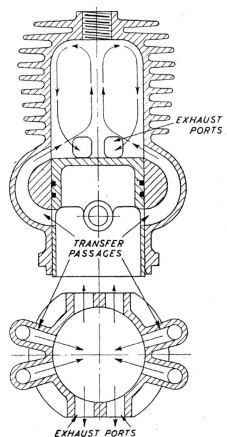

EXHAUST PORTS

TRANSFER PASSAGES

EXHAUST PORTS

design, and is complicated by so many incompatible factors that it is difficult to establish systematic rules for governing the area and timing of the ports. It will be fairly clear that the control of the ports by the piston imposes certain limitations on the timing, and prevents the best possible valve events from being obtained, but any other method of port control or valve gear entails a certain mechanical complication, and also an increase in the power

Fig. 22.—Diagram showing principle of "flat top" two-stroke engine

required to operate it. In nearly all cases so far, the addition of such mechanism has either failed to justify itself by the net increase in performance obtained, or has resulted in such complication of mechanism or construction as to render it undesirable or impracticable from the production point of view. This does not, however, rule out the possibility that some form of valve gear which shows an all-round improvement over the rather crude system of piston port control may not eventually be evolved. Control of individual ports, particularly the admission port and, to a lesser extent, the transfer port, by means of rotary or other types of valves, has produced promising results and is likely to increase in favour, according to present tendencies in the design of small engines within the scope of this book.

While it is very difficult, and perhaps even impossible, to arrive at a formula for port timing which can be guaranteed to give the most efficient results in any two-stroke engine, it is practicable to lay down fundamental rules, or at least recommendations, for port timing, which will produce reasonably good performance in practically all normally designed engines, and will serve as a basis for further experimental work. Several years ago, in response to many queries on this subject, the writer produced a " general purposes " timing diagram which has proved extremely helpful to many hundreds of two-stroke engine constructors, and can, therefore, be recommended with all confidence to readers of this book. This is shown in Fig. 23.

Variations or improvements on this timing system usually consist in increasing the depth of one or more of the ports to improve " breathing " at high speed, but when this is done it is advisable to make only a very slight alteration at a time and to check up carefully on the engine performance, to make certain that real improvement is obtained. Too deep an exhaust port results in the rejection of gases at an unnecessarily high pressure, and before all possible useful work has been extracted from them. The transfer port opening should not follow too closely on the heels of the exhaust port, or high-pressure gas may be forced down the passage, retarding the transfer of the charge, impairing the scavenging, and even tending to cause crankcase explosions. Too deep an admission port causes blowback through the carburettor and, apart from the wastage of fuel, this may actually defeat the object of promoting more efficient breathing and make good carburation difficult.

Even when all-round increased port depth is found to be conducive to higher efficiency at full speed, it may reduce flexibility, retard the rate of acceleration, or make starting more difficult, and in an engine designed for a particular duty, any of these factors may have as great a bearing on its practical utility as that of maximum performance. This does not even exclude the case of racing engines, because ability to accelerate quickly under load may be almost as important as speed in many cases. Port timing can never under any circumstances be " ideal " for all purposes, and the optimum qualities of any timing can only be realised under one particular set of conditions.

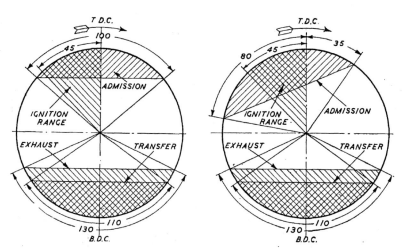

Fig. 23.—Typical timing diagrams for two-stroke engines with port admission and rotary-valve admission, respectively

The diagram shown above does not take into account the width of ports, in a direction at right angles to the piston stroke. It is advisable to make the total effective port width in all cases not less than twice the depth, excluding the width of any obstructions between subdivisions of a main port, such as port bars. This will produce ports of sufficient area for normal purposes in engines having approximately equal bore and stroke ; in engines of varying stroke/bore ratio, the width of port should be so related to the depth as to keep the port area constant for engines of a given displacement.

Increasing the width of the port may often be indulged without any ill effects and is, therefore, a desirable alternative to increasing the depth when tuning an engine for racing, but an excessively wide port weakens the cylinder wall and may locally affect cooling, producing a hot spot on the exhaust side and cold spots in the region of transfer and admission ports. Subdivision of the ports helps to counteract both faults, although two or three small ports have a less efficient discharge rate than a single port for a given total area. In an engine fitted with piston rings, individual ports must be kept sufficiently narrow to avoid risk of the rings jamming in them.

Port timing is most conveniently expressed in terms of percentage of the piston stroke, as its relation to crank angle may vary with the stroke/bore ratio, the connecting-rod length, and symmetry of the cylinder axis about the shaft centre line. Shortening the connecting rod relative to the piston stroke will increase the angular opening period of the exhaust and transfer ports in proportion to their depth and reduce the angular period of the admission port.

Desaxé Cylinder

When the cylinder axis is offset in relation to the crankshaft centre line, the relation between crank angle and port depth is further modified, and this effect can be put to good use in two-stroke engine design by increasing the dwell and retarding the closure of the exhaust and transfer ports. The effect is also beneficial from the mechanical point of view, as it enables the side thrust of the piston against the cylinder wall to be reduced during the power stroke ; there is, of course, a correspondingly equal increase of thrust on the compression stroke, but the load in this case is very much lower, so that the benefit is not cancelled out. Desaxé-cylinder engines suffer from the slight disadvantage that they are not capable of running with equal efficiency in either direction, as are engines having a symmetrical cylinder setting ; but this is not usually a very important objection. The offset should be in the direction of rotation and, whenever possible, the exhaust port should be on the side to which the cylinder is displaced. Several successful engines designed by the writer, including the " Kestrel " and the " Atom Minor," have had Desaxé cylinders.

Rotary Admission Valves

It has already been mentioned that the use of a timed valve has been applied with some advantage to the admission and occasionally the transfer port of a two-stroke engine. A full description of all the various methods employed, and the advantages thereby claimed or realised, cannot be included here, but briefly it may be stated that at least in the case of the admission port, valve control can be applied in an extremely simple manner and, due to the favourable conditions of

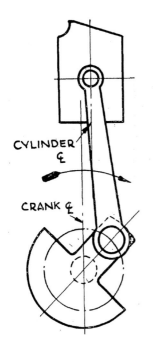

CYLINDER ℄

CRANK ℄

Fig. 24.—Diagram illustrating the **Desaxé** cylinder

working, is quite reliable and free from serious mechanical loss.

The simplest type of valve for this purpose is a rotary valve, which can be driven directly from the crankshaft and may even be incorporated in it, so that complication of working parts is avoided. A common arrangement consists of making the crankshaft hollow and cutting a port in its side, which registers at the appropriate time with a similar port cut in the main bearing. This simple device works quite well in many small engines, but it is evident that, from many points of view, the combination of an important load-carrying bearing with the valve is open to certain objections. The writer favours the use of a separate valve, driven by but not rigidly attached to the crankshaft, and capable of self-accommodation to its seating and adjustable for wear. A simple flat disc valve, driven by a fork or pin from the crankshaft, fulfils these conditions. Both the valve and its seating can be lapped or

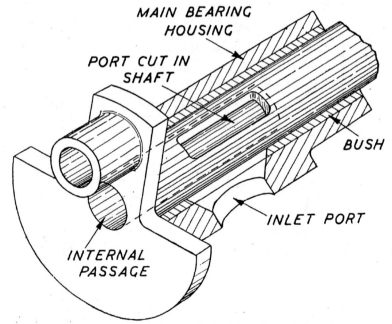

Fig. 25.—Rotary valve of the cylindrical or " crankshaft " type

otherwise finished to close mating accuracy, which is hardly affected by normal wear, as the parts are kept up to working contact by crankcase pressure, aided, if desired, by means of simple end-thrust adjustment.

The use of a rotary valve enables admission to be timed to maximum advantage, and large port openings can be employed without risk of blowback. Definite improvement in starting, normal running and maximum power can be produced in this way, and thus the all-round advantages of the rotary valve admission system are proved beyond question. The writer claims to be one of the first designers to incorporate rotary admission valves in small engines, and has used them successfully in the majority of his engines for aircraft, speed boats, stationary plant and motor-cycles for nearly twenty years past.

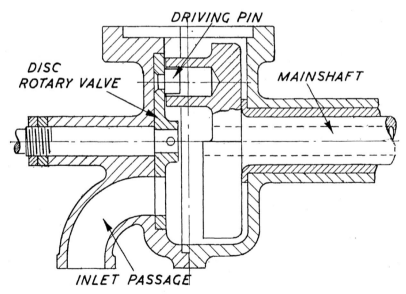

Fig. 26.—Disc type rotary valve

CHAPTER VI

EXAMPLES OF FOUR-STROKE ENGINES

ONE of the most successful model four-stroke engines produced by the writer is the 15-c.c. " Kiwi " engine, the description of which first appeared in *The Model Engineer* early in 1935. The essential features of this engine, which is illustrated in Fig. 27, and also the photograph published on page 82, are the straightforwardness of its design, and the facility with which its components can be machined with the limited equipment of the average model workshop. It has been a very popular design among constructors, and several hundred engines, either built to the exact design or with minor modifications and improvements, are known to have been produced for all kinds of purposes, including cruising and racing boats, stationary purposes and rail traction.

Although the engine was originally designed for general utility, with no claims to specially high performance, it proved to be a good deal more powerful than was anticipated, and soon became very popular for racing boats. One important factor in its success for this purpose was that it possessed sufficient stamina to retain its " tune " under the most arduous running conditions, a quality which was sadly lacking in many engines which had been designed specially for racing purposes.

For the reasons given above, no apologies are considered necessary for including this somewhat antique design in this book ; not only is it a very suitable design for the first effort of the novice, but it also has a wide field of utility and, if reasonably well made will work reliably over many hundreds

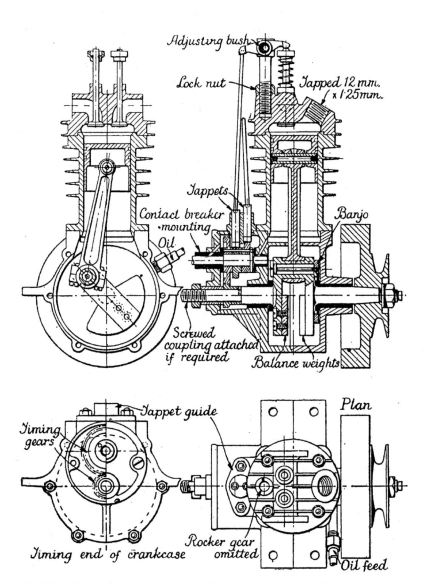

Fig. 27.—General arrangement of "Kiwi" engine, 15 c.c. four-strcke 1 in. 1⅛ in. stroke, introduced early in 1935

The original " Kiwi " 15 c.c engine

of working hours, with little liability to mechanical trouble or breakdown.

The general design of this engine may be said to follow motor-cycle practice ; it has the characteristic type of crank-case divided on the vertical centre line, with the timing gear housed in an extension of one side member, but not containing the usual internal flywheels, as these necessitate an unduly bulky crankcase and tend to increase the all-on weight of the engine. The crankshaft is in one piece, either machined from the solid or fabricated by brazing, the former being recommended, and not by any means a formidable task, as it can be made from rectangular steel bar, with balance weights afterwards bolted on. A bronze connecting rod, with split big-end bearing, is fitted. The cylinder is normally adapted for air-cooling, though it may be water-jacketed if desired, and the head is of straightforward design, with vertical valves and simple rocker levers with eccentric bush adjustment to take up tappet clearance.

It may be said that the " Kiwi " engine represents sound four-stroke engine design boiled down to its simplest essentials ; but there was never any doubt that some of the features in its design were not the most suitable for high efficiency performance, and in view of the demand for a good racing engine, experimental modifications were made to the original engine, with a view to improving it in this respect. A new cylinder head was designed, incorporating inclined valves and larger valve ports, and an automatic lubrication system was fitted. After these new features had been fully tested out on the test bench and in practical service, they were then incorporated in an entirely new design intended specially for high-efficiency work.

The " Kittiwake " Engine

Fig. 28 shows the results of this experimental research. It will be seen that the general constructional features of the " Kiwi " engine are retained, but the working parts are more robust, and the crankshaft runs on ball bearings. A more roomy timing case is provided, to accommodate more sturdy timing gears and high-efficiency cams, and an extension on the lower part of the crankcase forms an oil sump and houses the oil pump, which is driven by worm gearing from the crankshaft. The cylinder head has valves inclined at an included angle of 60 degrees, operated by offset rockers, which, together with the push rods, are enclosed and lubricated by oil mist. These features make the construction of the engine more difficult, and also add a substantial amount to the weight and complexity of the engine, but all this is fully justified, and, indeed, essential if the utmost amount of power and stamina is required. Many engines of this type have been constructed and employed successfully in racing boats. An enlarged version of the design has also been produced to suit Inter-

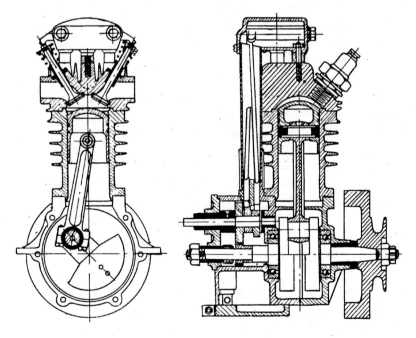

Fig. 28.—General arrangement of the 15 c.c. capacity " Kittiwake " engine

An example of the "Kittiwake" 15 c.c. engine, constructed by Mr. H. Scamell

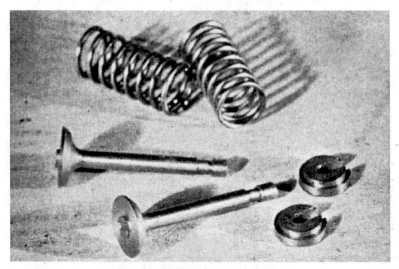

Valves and springs for Wall o.h.v. engine

national class racing boats, in which the capacity limit is 30 cubic centimetres.

The " Apex Minor " Engine

While the conventional lines of full-size practice have been successfully exploited in the above engines, experiments have also been made in less orthodox forms of design, with the object of securing the utmost compactness of bulk and economy in weight. The " Apex " engines embody the use of overhung crank and a cross-camshaft driven by skew gearing. Except for a plain blank endplate, the crankcase is entirely in one piece, incorporating the main bearing and camshaft bearing housings, and other components also show a marked departure from generally accepted practice. On this account, perhaps, they have been less popular than the " Kiwi " and " Kittiwake " engines, but there is no question of their practical success, and certain advantages in construction are obtained in their design.

The " Apex Minor " 15-c.c. engine is the best-known in this class, and is illustrated in Fig. 29. It has the same bore and stroke as the " Kiwi " engine, but has hardly anything else in common with this or other orthodox types of engines. The overhung crankshaft runs in a ball race at its inner end, and a sleeve bush at the outer end, the skew timing pinion being

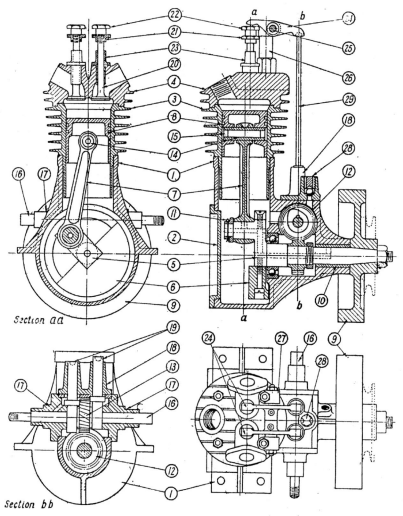

Section aa

Section bb

Fig. 29.—General arrangement of 15·c.c. " Apex Minor " engine

G

located between the two and driving the camshaft, located
above and at right angles to the main shaft centre. No base
flange is provided on the cylinder, which is located by its
skirt fitting an upper extension of the crankcase casting, and
secured by four long studs, which also pass right through the
cylinder head. Vertical valves with up-swept ports are

An " Apex Minor " 15 c.c. engine, constructed by Mr. H. Hayhurst

employed, the rockers being of the plain lever type, operated
through push rods from tappets with flat feet bearing directly
on the cams. These principles of construction result in a
compact and rigid engine, which is not only economical in
structural material—in other words, of low weight for a given
capacity and power—but also has the minimum number of
components for an overhead-valve four-stroke engine.

The " Kinglet " Engine

Although the great majority of model four-stroke engines
have been of the overhead-valve type, there is much to be
said in favour of the side-valve engine in cases where the duty
is moderate and the utmost reliability is desired. Owing to
their effect on the shape of the combustion chamber, side

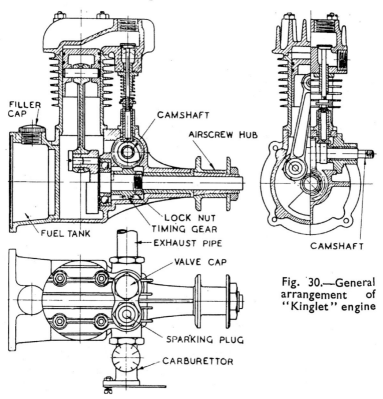

FILLER CAP

CAMSHAFT

AIRSCREW HUB

LOCK NUT
TIMING GEAR

EXHAUST PIPE

FUEL TANK

VALVE CAP

CAMSHAFT

SPARKING PLUG

CARBURETTOR

Fig. 30.—General
arrangement of
"Kinglet" engine

valves rather tend to restrict the use of high compression ratios and also the extent to which an engine can be tuned for high performance ; but, on the other hand, they simplify the valve gear, reduce the number of working parts and enable a more compact engine, especially in respect of vertical height, to be produced. The valve gear can be made to work comparatively quietly and will generally work for much longer periods without adjustment than overhead valve gear.

One of the most popular side-valve engines produced by the writer is the 5-c.c. " Kinglet " engine, which, in spite of its very small size, is very consistent in performance and has remarkable flexibility of control. It will be seen from Fig. 30 that the general mechanical design is developed from that of the " Apex " engines, but a totally different cylinder is employed, having an aluminium head with valve pockets cast into it on the port side. The cylinder and head are held down

The original " Kinglet " 5 c.c. side-valve engine

by four long studs anchored in the top of the crankcase. This engine is sufficiently light in weight to be capable of employment for aircraft propulsion, but has been more popular for light-weight marine craft, and in at least one case it has been modified by the fitting of an overhead-valve cylinder head for use in a racing boat.

Horizontal Engines

The type of engine which has for very many years been employed for stationary work in full-size practice, that is, the horizontal water-cooled open-crank engine, has always been a popular prototype for model constructors, and sets of castings and parts for the construction of engines of this type in various sizes have long been featured by several model supply firms. In many cases these engines have been coupled to

The engine of the " M.E." road roller, constructed by Mr. J. Ripper

generators or incorporated in other types of miniature power plants, and the possibility of using them for practical work, such as accumulator charging, has been demonstrated.

Of recent years, however, attention has been mainly directed to the construction of high-performance engines, and in consequence, the popularity of such engines has tended to decline, but there is a good deal of scope for their development on up-to-date lines, and for performance a good deal more exacting than that which could be handled by the older and relatively slow-speed engines. An example of a horizontal engine which, while not designed for stationary work, is very well suited for it, is the 15-c.c. Aveling-type Road Roller engine shown in Plate I. This is adapted from the prototype so as to resemble it in general character and appearance, although the latter is a compression-ignition engine which runs on crude oil, features hardly practicable in the model, which is therefore designed to run on petrol. The appearance of the engine is attractive, and it will be seen that the main working parts are totally enclosed, so that they can be efficiently lubricated and run at much higher speeds than are desirable for an open engine.

The water jacket of this engine is surmounted by an open-topped hopper, which holds sufficient water to enable fairly long runs to be made without replacement, but, if desired, the top of the hopper may be closed and an extra water tank with circulating pipes fitted, in which case the engine may be run continuously as long as may be required. Lubrication is automatic, and the supply of oil in the sump will last for several hours' running.

Multi-Cylinder Engines

As a general rule, the single-cylinder engine is by far the most satisfactory type in small sizes in respect of actual performance and reliability, but it is by no means impossible to build satisfactory engines of more than one cylinder, and the very fact that they involve extra problems of design and

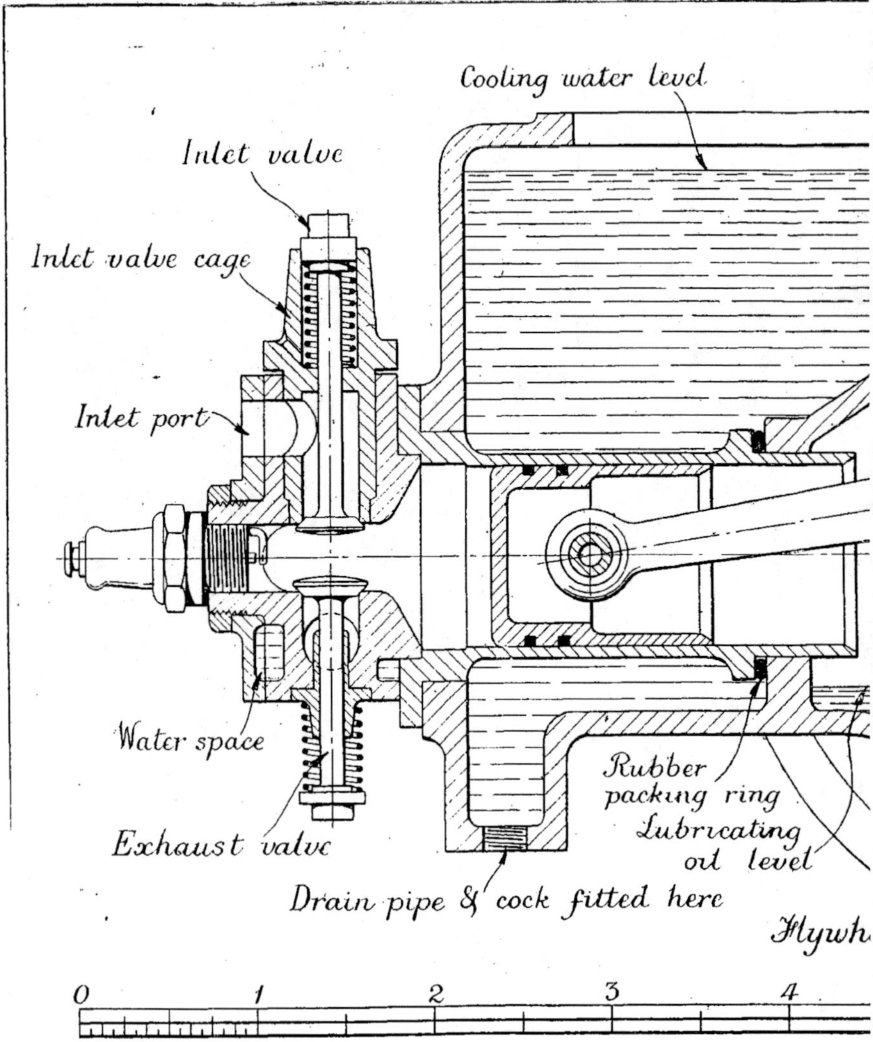

Percival Marshall & Co., Ltd., London

Cooling water level

Inlet valve

Inlet valve cage

Inlet port

Water space

Exhaust valve

Rubber
packing ring
Lubricating
oil level

Flywh

Drain pipe & cock fitted here

0   1   2   3   4

Plate I.—Longitudinal section of 15 c.c. hopper-cooled engine for " M.E." road roller (full size).

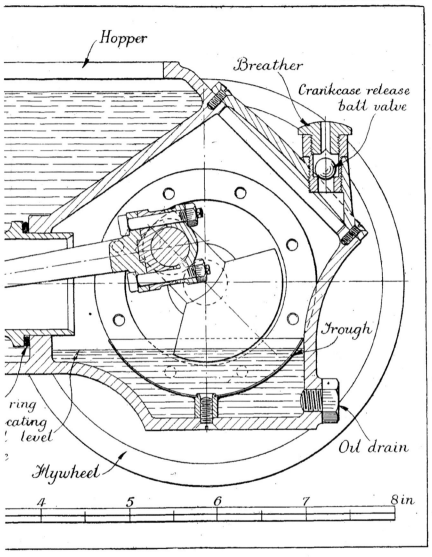

Hopper

Breather

Crankcase release
ball valve

Trough

Oil drain

ring
cating
level

Flywheel

4   5   6   7   8 in

construction is in many cases an added incentive to attempt the task.

Several very successful twin-cylinder engines have been constructed, including examples of flat twin engines, which have always held a fascination for petrol engine constructors. A 12-c.c. water-cooled engine of this type, fabricated entirely from stock rod, sheet and tube material, built up by silver-soldering, has been produced by Mr. F. G. Arkell, a pioneer of model petrol engines, and used very successfully for the pro-

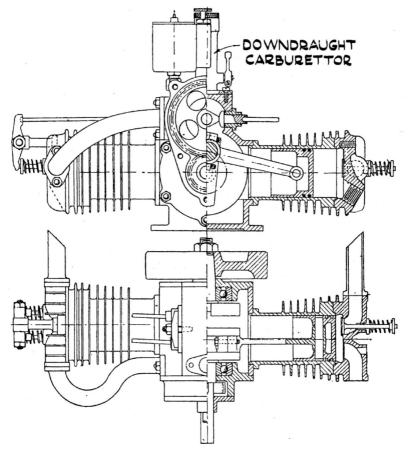

Fig. 31.—A 30 c.c. flat twin engine designed by the writer

MODEL PETROL ENGINES

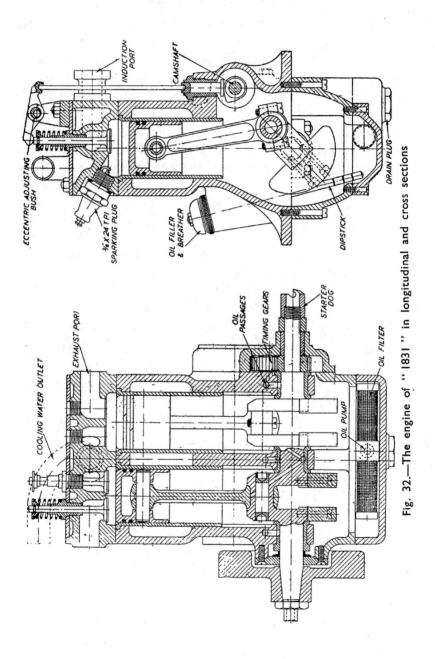

Fig. 32.—The engine of " 1831 " in longitudinal and cross sections

pulsion of a model cabin cruiser. Other flat twin engines have
been used for model aircraft and speed-boat propulsion, where
their advantages in shape and weight distribution are obvious ;
but, so far as can be ascertained, their performance is practically always inferior to that of the single-cylinder engine.
An interesting vertical twin water-cooled engine of .30 cc.
capacity has been designed by the writer for the I.C. engine-
driven $3\frac{1}{2}$-in. gauge locomotive " 1831," and has been proved
by actual test to be highly satisfactory in general performance.
It is equally suitable for application to other duties, particularly that of propelling a fairly large model power boat. This
engine is illustrated in Fig. 32, and it will be seen that its
design follows fairly orthodox lines, but it is by no means
devoid of interesting and distinctive features. The main
component is a monobloc casting embracing the upper half of
the crankcase and the jackets for the two cylinders, in which
steel or cast-iron " wet " liners are inserted. The crankshaft

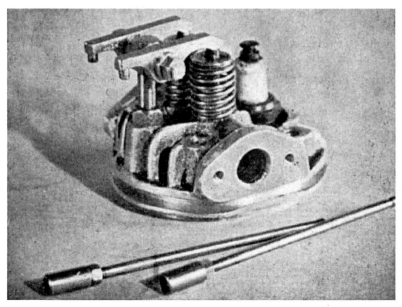

Cylinder head for Wall o.h.v. engine

One of the latest "Wall" 30 c.c. o.h.v. four-cylinder engines

Percival Marshall & Co., Ltd., London

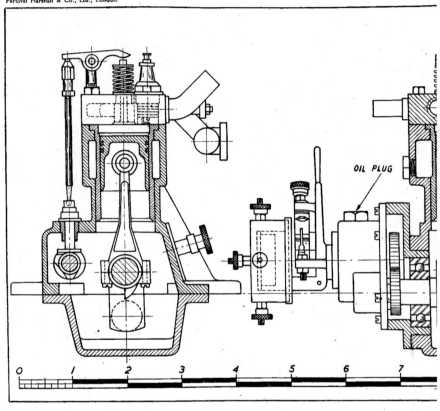

OIL PLUG

Plate II.—General arrangement of one of the " Wall " four-cylinder engines

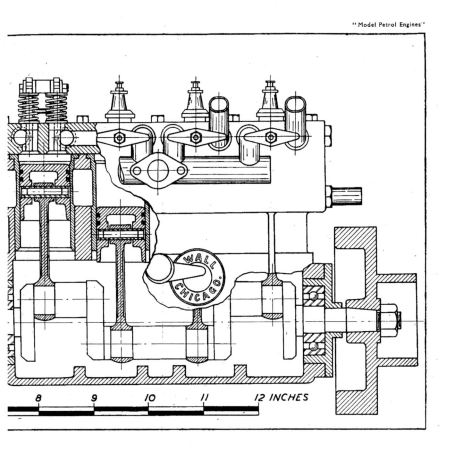

8   9   10   11   12 INCHES

is made from solid steel bar, with attached balance weights, and both crankpins are in the same plane, so that the pistons move simultaneously in the same direction, the power impulses being evenly spaced at 360 degrees. A monobloc head, having cored water passages so that all parts are adequately cooled, is fitted, and the valves are disposed vertically, operated by rockers and push rods from flat tappets working directly on the cams. Lubrication is by means of a gearwheel pump, and the sump has an adequate oil capacity for long continuous runs. A high-tension distributor for coil ignition is fitted to the camshaft, and a specially-designed carburettor, which gives a wide margin of control, is employed. The engine drives the locomotive through a centrifugal clutch and variable friction drive transmission system.

Four-cylinder engines of small dimensions have, up to the present, been extremely rare, and there is no doubt that the problems involved in their construction are momentous, but the practicability of producing small engines of this type, down to a total displacement of 30 c.c., have been demonstrated. Mr. Elmer Wall, of Chicago, has produced both side-valve and overhead-valve engines of 50 c.c. and 30 c.c. having four cylinders and conforming generally in design and appearance to the conventional type of motor-car engine. The Wall 30-c.c. engine is illustrated on page 96.

Perhaps the greatest achievement on record in the construction of working model multi-cylinder engines is that of Mr. Gerald Smith, who, following up an early success with a five-cylinder radial engine, produced some years ago an outstanding example of fine design and workmanship in the shape of an eighteen-cylinder double-banked radial engine having cylinders $1\frac{3}{8}$ in. bore by $1\frac{1}{2}$ in. stroke. The total capacity of this engine was approximately 450 c.c., very much larger than that of any engine employed in the type of model aircraft likely to be built by the average model engineer.

CHAPTER VII

EXAMPLES OF TWO-STROKE ENGINES

ALTHOUGH the smaller sizes of model petrol engines developed in recent years have been almost exclusively of the two-stroke type, it would be hardly correct to assume that the general design of such engines has made progress commensurate with their advance in popularity. There is a somewhat depressing monotony about the design of these engines and, although definite advances in the performance have undoubtedly been achieved, these have been due more to improvement in construction than any new departures in design. Some constructors are of the opinion that, in engines of such extreme mechanical simplicity, there is hardly any scope for new ideas in design, but the writer does not share this opinion, and in each of the many two-stroke engines he has produced, an attempt has been made to incorporate some new feature or principle of design ; a policy which has undoubtedly proved to be justified in practice, if only for the simple reason that the exploration and test of the various ideas tried out has led to the accumulation of much valuable data on design.

The " Atom " Engines

Some twenty years ago the writer designed and constructed a 52-c.c. engine which was known as the "Atom," though its size was very large compared to that of most popular model two-stroke engines at the present day. This engine was intended for the propulsion of model aircraft and, although it was never actually used for this purpose, it was proved by bench tests to be of a suitable type and ample power output,

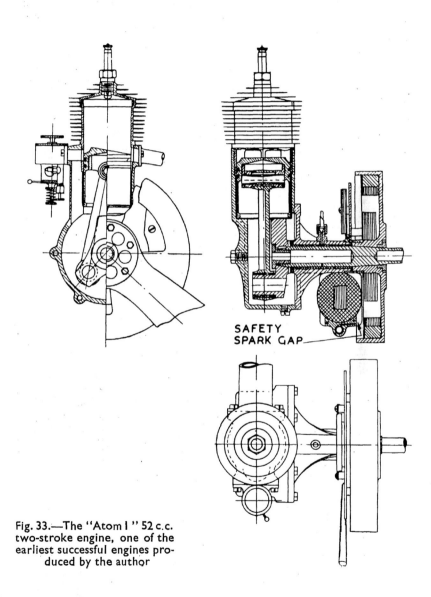

SAFETY
SPARK GAP

Fig. 33.—The "Atom I" 52 c.c.
two-stroke engine, one of the
earliest successful engines produced by the author

The " Atom I " engine produced in 1925

though the desirability of producing a much smaller engine, to suit model aircraft of manageable size, was fully realised. About this time, however, attention was directed to the use of model petrol engines for speed-boat propulsion and, after some trials of the above engine in a hull, a design was produced for an engine conforming to the International class limit of

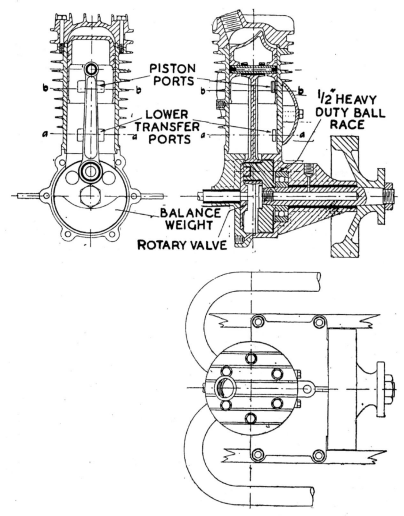

PISTON PORTS

LOWER TRANSFER PORTS

½" HEAVY DUTY BALL RACE

BALANCE WEIGHT

ROTARY VALVE

Fig. 34.—The 30 c.c. "Atom III" engine

30 c.c. for racing boats. This incorporated some of the features of the " Atom " engine, and was known, therefore, as " Atom II " ; it was fairly successful, but in the course of a particularly exacting bench test, a mechanical failure took place which indicated the need for modification of the design. As a result, a third engine, known as " Atom III," was constructed, and achieved all that had been intended in its design, with a very high standard of mechanical reliability and consistent performance. The main features of " Atom III " were its extremely rigid structural design and ample bearings to cope with heavy duty and high speed ; a cast-iron cylinder having twin exhaust ports and a detachable transfer passage ; and a detachable aluminium head, well finned externally and designed internally to promote efficient combustion. A rotary admission valve was employed, and provision made for positive lubrication by crankcase pressure, to feed control valves on the main bearing and cylinder wall. A fairly

The " Atom III " 30 c.c. speed boat engine

large number of these machines were made by constructors, both in this country and abroad, and used with success in model speed boats.

"Atom IV" was also a 30-c.c. engine, but in this case a reversion to model aircraft requirements called for light-weight construction, no other special features being incorporated, and in view of the need for still smaller engines for this duty, not much progress was made with this engine.

The latest development of this class of engines, "Atom V," is also intended principally for model speed-boat propulsion. It resembles "Atom III" in mechanical design, but has an

An example of the "Atom V" engine constructed by Mr. J. Powell

H

entirely redesigned cylinder, in which the exhaust ports are in two sets diametrically opposed, and two sets of transfer ports, each with a detachable cover, are similarly opposed at right angles to them. Rotary valve admission is again employed, the induction passage being of special design to facilitate easy flow of mixture at high speed. Provision is made in the design for the fitting of a metering oil pump for positive pressure lubrication, and a self-winding drum and ratchet starting gear.

Another view of Mr. Powell's " Atom V " engine

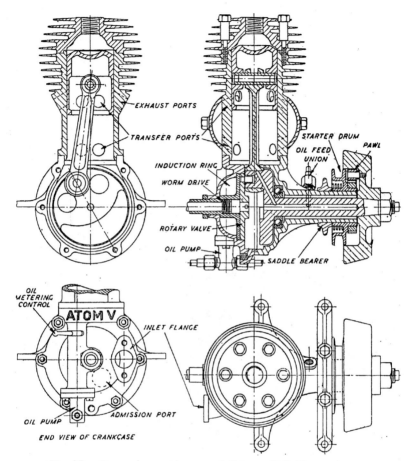

Fig. 35.—General arrangement of "Atom V" 30 c.c. engine

"Atom Minor" Engines

The first of the writer's engines to be successfully employed for model aircraft propulsion was the 15-c.c. "Atom Minor" engine, designed and produced in 1932, after some preliminary experiments with a Wall 25-c.c. engine, in collaboration with Captain C. E. Bowden. It may justly be claimed that the "Atom Minor" was the first engine to demonstrate the possibilities of reasonably small power-driven model aircraft.

In the design of the " Atom Minor " engine, illustrated in Plate III, many of the constructional principles of the larger " Atom " engines are embodied, including the sturdy shaft and bearings, which had been found desirable by intensive testing on the bench and in actual service. Although intended

Side view of the original 15 c c. " Atom Minor " engine, produced by the author in 1932 for model aircraft experiments in collaboration with Captain C. E. Bowden

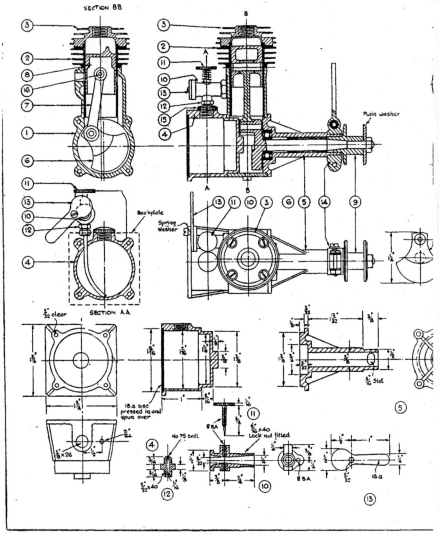

Plate III.—The "Atom Minor" 6 c.c. two-stroke engine

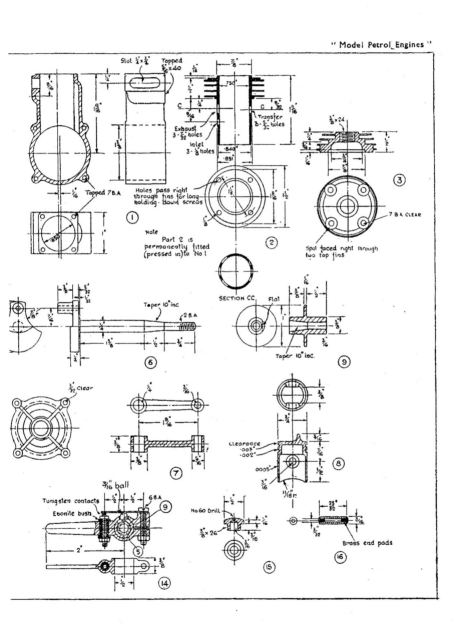

as a light-weight engine, no flimsiness of construction was considered permissible. The crankcase barrel and cylinder housing were cast in one piece, with a thin inserted cast-iron liner, and a finned aluminium head was attached by four

Front view of the 15 c.c. "Atom Minor" engine

studs. Both the front and rear sides of the crankcase were
faced, and provided with bolting lugs for the attachment of
the main bearing housing and rear cover respectively, these
being interchangeable for the purpose of adapting the engine
to run in either direction. As the cylinder centre was Desaxé,
the engine was not capable of running at full efficiency in
either direction without this provision.

The " Atom Minor " in its standard form was not equipped
with rotary valve admission, but had the usual inlet port in
the cylinder wall. The carburettor employed was of the mixing
valve type, provided with a throttle valve, and capable of a

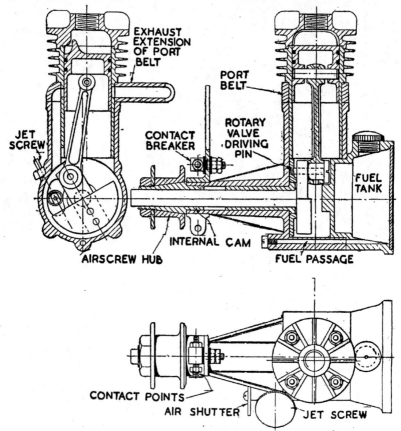

Fig. 36.—The " Kestrel " 5 c.c. engine

wide range of speed control, but float feed carburettors of various types have also been employed. A simple form of pivoted rocker contact-breaker, capable of being dismantled without tools, was fitted on the main bearing housing and operated by a cam formed on the back of the airscrew hub. The weight of the standard engine, including a 15-in. Elektron airscrew, was 17½ ozs.

A later edition of the 15-c.c. "Atom Minor" had several minor modifications in design, including the use of ball races for the main crankshaft journal bearings, and was in production for some time by Messrs. A. E. Jones Ltd.

In response to the demand for engines of smaller capacity for model aircraft propulsion, the "Atom Minor" was at a

The original 5 c.c. "Kestrel" two-stroke engine

later date redesigned and produced in much smaller form, the main characteristics of the original design being retained as far as possible. In this engine, known as the " New Atom Minor," a combination of ball race and sleeve bush is used for the main crankshaft bearing ; the capacity is 6 c.c. This engine is illustrated in Plate III.

The " Kestrel " Engine

As a result of further experiments in two-stroke engine design, undertaken particularly with a view to producing an efficient and simple engine suitable for construction by amateurs with limited equipment, the " Kestrel " 5-c.c. engine was produced in 1937. In this engine, rotary valve admission is employed, the valve being located in the front of the crankcase, between the crankcase wall and the crank web. The carburettor is integral with the crankcase casting, and no external fuel pipe is used. Following an idea tried tentatively in the " New Atom Minor," the fuel tank is incorporated in the rear crankcase endplate, and communication with the carburettor jet is established by way of a drilled passage. Another innovation in the design is the use of a port belt containing exhaust and transfer passages, which is pressed on to the centre of the cylinder, and serves to simplify a part of the construction which often involves difficulty for the inexperienced engine builder.

The popularity of this engine among constructors may be judged from the fact that several hundreds of sets of castings have been sold, and many of the finished engines have been successfully employed in model aircraft, power boats and racing cars, some of them with outstanding success. Several modifications and near-imitations of the design have also been produced.

As in the case of the four-stroke engine, comparatively few model two-strokes have been made with more than one cylinder, and still less with more than two cylinders. In the case of the two-stroke, the necessity for pre-compression of the

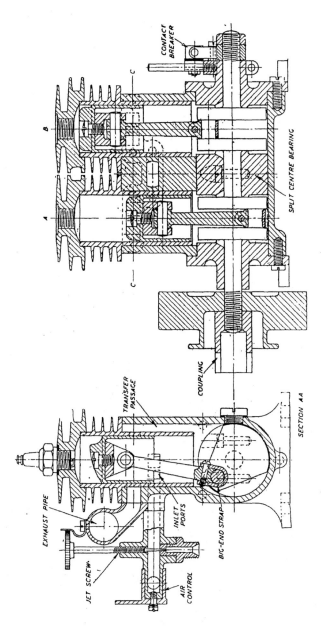

Fig. 37.—Sections of 6 c.c " Curwen " twin two-stroke engine

charge in the crankcase makes the construction of the latter more than usually difficult, as each individual crank chamber must be pressure-sealed. Successful twin two-strokes have, however, been made as small as 6 c.c., and there is at least one example of a three-cylinder engine in existence, constructed by Mr. D. Stanger, a pioneer in model aircraft engines, who for many years held the record for duration of flight with a petrol driven model aeroplane.

The examples of engines illustrated in this and the preceding chapter are intended principally for the guidance of readers in the application of features and principles of design which have been discussed earlier in the book, and there is no claim that they exhaust the possibilities for original design, or represent the ultimate development along any particular line.

The Stanger 15 c.c. three-cylinder two-stroke engine.

CHAPTER VIII

CARBURATION

IN all internal combustion engines running on liquid fuel, some means must be provided of supplying an exactly controlled quantity of fuel in a finely-divided or vaporised form, so that it can be brought into intimate contact with the air necessary to support combustion. Compression-ignition or " Diesel " engines employ mechanical methods of metering and spraying the fuel, but in practically all engines which consume light, volatile fuels of low flash point, the simplest and most convenient method of introducing the fuel is to mix it with the air taken into the engine. When the air is thus " carburetted " with the correct proportion of fuel, it forms a combustible mixture, which is readily ignited by means of an electric spark, and the speed and power of the engine can be controlled by varying the quantity of mixture admitted, so long as the ratio of fuel to air remains within certain limits (which vary with different fuels) known as the " combustible range."

The device by means of which the admixture of air and fuel is effected, in other words, the " carburettor," has the rather exacting triple duty of spraying the fuel very finely, metering it correctly to suit the quantity of air, and controlling the amount of air-fuel mixture to suit the immediate needs of the engine. In full-size practice, more or less elaborate and complicated carburettors are used, according to the degree of control, economy and efficiency demanded of the engine, but in smaller engines it becomes desirable, if not absolutely necessary, to simplify the carburettor, even at the expense of some of its refinements. Generally speaking, carburation difficulties become more acute as the size of the engine decreases, for, although it is easy enough to spray the fuel finely, metering control in very small jet orifices is not so easy. A large proportion of failures and running troubles in model petrol engines are due to incorrect carburation, and the finest engine in the world cannot possibly give its best performance if it is not constantly fed with the correct proportions of fuel and air for efficient combustion.

In its most elementary form, a carburettor consists simply of a fuel jet, or capillary orifice, let into an air passage in such a way that any fuel which emerges from the jet is carried away and mixed with the air which travels through the passage. The fuel jet is very commonly disposed at right angles to the air passage, in the manner shown in Fig. 39, but it may also be arranged parallel, or at an angle—even, in certain cases, opposed to the latter. The methods of feeding both the air and fuel may vary considerably, but in the majority of cases, the air is drawn through the passage by atmospheric displacement, so that the pressure in it is slightly lower than that of the outside atmosphere, and the resultant depression or "suction" is also utilised to draw the fuel from the jet. There are, however, exceptions to this rule ; air may be forced through the carburettor under pressure in certain types of supercharged or " forced induction " engines, and fuel may be fed to the jet under gravity or any desired degree of pressure. Any deviation from the normal method of feeding, however, involves complication of the carburettor, and is likely to increase carburettor difficulties rather than otherwise, so that it is hardly to be encouraged unless some very urgent aim is in view in model petrol engines.

If the air travels slowly through the passage, the suction effect on the fuel will be very slight, and for a given size of jet orifice only a small quantity of fuel will emerge. Moreover, it will do little more than creep along the wall of the pipe, so that it does not become atomised or mix intimately with the air.

By increasing the velocity of air through the pipe, however, the fuel is drawn from the jet so vigorously as to be thrown into a fine spray, which is carried away in suspension by the air and, if sufficiently volatile, partly vaporised as well. This state of things is highly desirable for good carburation, and thus the air passage or " mixing chamber " of the carburettor must be made sufficiently small in diameter in relation to the displacement of the engine, to ensure that air passes through it at high velocity, at the lowest speed at which the engine is required to run. It is not, however, desirable to restrict the bore of the entire induction passage, as this would set up undesirable skin friction and adversely affect the " breathing " efficiency of the engine ; so the bore is usually restricted locally, forming a " choke tube " in which the air moves at its maximum velocity. If the passage is well designed, very little throttling need take place in the choke tube ; the most efficient method is to taper it both ways, so that sudden

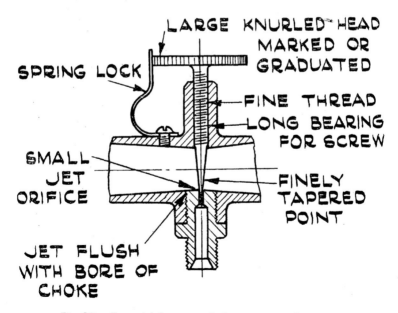

Fig. 38.—Essential features of elementary carburettor

changes of diameter are avoided. The highest possible coefficient of discharge is obtained by using a carefully shaped " venturi " tube, and the jet orifice should be located at or near the point of minimum diameter or " throat."

Although it is practicable in certain circumstances to employ a fixed jet orifice, the size of this would be very minute in a small model engine, and could only be determined by actual test. It is therefore more convenient to employ a variable jet, controlled by a tapered needle which can be moved in or out of the orifice to control the effective area ; and the most popular means of operating the needle is by means of a knurled screw, as shown in Fig. 38. If some form of air shutter is fitted to the intake end of the air passage, means are thus available for controlling the quantities of both fuel and air, and the resultant device is, theoretically at any rate, capable of performing all the necessary functions of a complete carburettor. In the great majority of really small petrol engines, such a carburettor may do, and often does, all that is normally required of it in practice.

Methods of Fuel Feeding

The means by which the fuel is supplied to the jet have a very important effect on carburation control. If the fuel is fed by a gravity from a tank above its own level, the flow of fuel will be to some extent independent of the depression in the air passage, and even when the engine stops the flow will continue. Unless some automatic cut-off device is fitted, this is almost a fatal objection to the use of direct gravity feed, as it is very liable to flood the engine before it can be started, and at the best will make it difficult to find correct initial jet adjustment. Increasing the fuel feed pressure by raising the tank level, or by artificial pressure, will accentuate this condition and, although direct pressure feed has been used very successfully on certain racing engines, it renders adjustment extremely critical, and is not to be recommended to the average user. If the supply tank is located below the level of the jet, however, the discharge from the jet depends entirely on the suction in the air passage, and ceases automatically when the engine stops. As this method is the simplest and most " foolproof," it is very commonly employed on model engines, but it is not without certain disadvantages, to be discussed later. It is important to remember that the method of fuel feeding has an important effect on the performance of the carburettor, and the same carburettor may give totally different results by changing the mode of feeding.

Constant-Head Control

In view of the influence of any change of fuel pressure or " head " on the output of the jet, it follows that in any simple gravity or suction fuel supply system, the difference of level in the fuel tank caused as the fuel is gradually used up, will

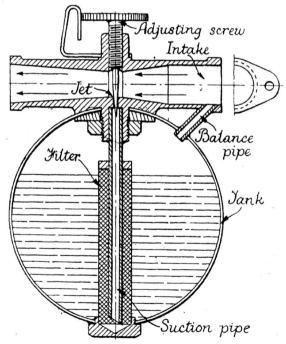

Fig. 39.—Suction carburettor fitted directly to fuel tank with internal sleeve filter and pressure-balancing pipe

cause the mixture to become steadily weaker. This effect can be minimised by making the tank as shallow as possible, and in very small engines, this expedient serves the purpose fairly well if a moderate exactitude of fuel adjustment can be tolerated. But in larger engines, where any considerable amount of fuel must be carried in the tank, and particularly in the case of mobile power plants which may be subject to rocking or change of trim, this method becomes impracticable, and it is therefore necessary to introduce some method of controlling the effect of variable head on the fuel feed adjustment.

The most popular method of ensuring a constant head on the jet from a gravity or low-pressure supply system is the well-known " float feed," which works on precisely the same principle as the " ball cock " in the cistern of a domestic water supply system. Instead of taking the fuel directly from the main tank, it is allowed first to flow into a subsidiary ready-use reservoir, known as the float chamber, which contains the control mechanism. This consists of a float to which is attached, either directly or through a system of levers, a valve which controls the flow of fuel from the main reservoir to the chamber.

When the latter is empty, this valve is open, so that the fuel flows in freely, but as the level in the chamber rises, the float lifts and gradually closes the valve, so that, when a certain level is reached, the supply is cut off entirely. This level is generally adjusted so as to prevent the fuel overflowing from the carburettor jet, but at the same time to keep it sufficiently high to require very little suction to lift it. As the fuel is discharged from the jet, the float controls the ingress of fuel, so that it is maintained substantially at the same level all the time the engine is running. The precision of control depends upon the design and workmanship of the float valve mechanism.

The simplest form of float feed is that in which the float is attached directly to the valve, either in fixed or adjustable relation to it, so that it closes upwardly as the float rises. If the entry of fuel is at the top of the chamber, a valve consisting of a conical-ended spindle, projecting from the top of the float and working in a coned seating in the chamber cover, will serve the required purpose. Alternatively, the fuel may be admitted at the bottom of the chamber, in which case the valve is of the " inverted " type, consisting of a spindle with an enlarged conical head, working in a seating on the outside of the supply orifice. The latter method is a little more elaborate in construction, but generally more convenient in installation and use, as it enables the float chamber cover to be removed for inspection of the float action without disconnecting the fuel pipe. It is also more accurate and reliable, because in the " top feed " system the fuel

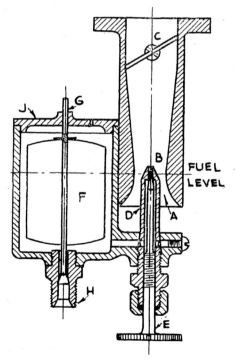

Fig. 40.—Simple float-feed vertical carburettor

entering the chamber flows over the float and thereby affects
its buoyancy. Both these simple systems, however, are used
successfully in model petrol engine carburettors, sometimes
with minor variations.

In passing, it may be mentioned that the type of float gear
used in full-sized carburettors generally incorporates an
indirect operation of the float valve by a system of levers,
usually above the float and attached to the chamber cover.
This method can be adapted to model engines, but as the
direct-operated valve can be made to work quite satisfactorily,
such elaboration is usually considered unnecessary. Float
feed has been applied to engines as small as $2\frac{1}{2}$ c.c., but is not
usually found on engines smaller than about 10 to 15 c.c. In
engines of larger sizes it is considered highly desirable if exact
control of carburation is desired.

It is possible to control the head of fuel more or less
accurately without using a float by means of what is called
the "bird-feed" system, illustrated in Fig. 41. In this system
the main fuel tank has no air vent in the top, so that air can
only enter to replace the fuel used by passing up the tube
communicating with the subsidiary chamber. Consequently,
when the end of this pipe is submerged, the main tank becomes
" air locked," and no fuel can flow out of it until the end of the
pipe is again exposed. This system has been used with some

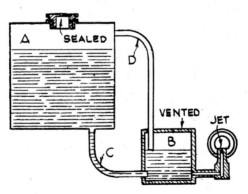

Fig. 41.—Bird-feed fuel supply system

success for model carburettors, but has never been really popular, as it is less accurate than float feed and liable to be upset by vibration or rocking of the plant.

To assist the flow of petrol when it is not convenient to elevate the main tank, a low air pressure is sometimes applied to the tank. The simplest method of doing this is to use a rubber bladder, which is blown up by an inflator or by the mouth to a pressure not exceeding two or three pounds to the square inch. This method works quite reliably, but it is important that the bladder should be of ample air capacity —several times the capacity of the tank—and that it should always be blown up to a constant pressure. Too high an air pressure may result in interference with proper float action ; with top feed, it may tend to force the valve off its seating, and with bottom feed, it may prevent it from opening.

Petrol Pumps

Several model racing engines have been fitted with fuel pumps to raise the fuel from a low-level tank. If these are used in conjunction with float feed, the discharge pressure must be very delicately controlled, for the reasons given above. It is generally more convenient to dispense with the float and fit the chamber with a spill pipe which allows excess fuel to return to the tank after a pre-determined level has been reached.

The most satisfactory type of pump for lifting fuel appears to be one of the diaphragm type, operated by a cam, as extensively employed in motor-car practice. As only a very small quantity of fuel has to be dealt with, the pump should be geared to run at a low speed, so that it works reliably and takes very little power. Reciprocating plunger pumps are not highly suitable for this purpose, owing to the difficulty in keeping the plungers properly sealed and lubricated when dealing with a very light liquid, and most forms of rotary pumps are subject to similar objections—and others which need not be discussed—when used for this particular purpose.

Mixture Compensation

When the speed of the air through the choke tube of a carburettor varies for any reason, the discharge of fuel from the jet, and also the atomisation of fuel, is affected to some extent. If the fuel supply has been adjusted by means of the jet needle or a calibrated jet has been fitted, to produce the correct mixture at a given speed, it will tend to become richer as the speed increases, and weaker as it is reduced ; this assumes that the jet works under suction, and neglects the effect of supplying the fuel directly to the jet by gravity or pressure, as this modifies the rate of flow in a manner which has already been discussed.

The rate of air flow through the carburettor is not solely dependent upon the speed of the engine, but may be varied either by throttling or alteration of load. Thus any engine which is subject to varying load or is controlled by means of a throttle in the induction pipe is subject to fluctuation of the mixture strength. If the engine, under its normal running conditions, can be kept at a fairly constant load and speed, the strength of the mixture, as supplied by a simple form of carburettor, may not alter sufficiently to cause misfiring or other serious trouble ; it is also possible to cope with wide variation in both respects by manual adjustment of air or fuel supply, or both. But when good carburation, over a wide range of running conditions, and with the simplest possible control, is essential, the mixture must be compensated by automatic means to correct discrepancies caused in this way.

The devices employed to produce automatic mixture compensation are many and varied, but all of them operate by controlling the supply of either the air or the fuel, or both, and are actuated either mechanically from the throttle control or by the engine suction.

Mechanical compensation has been employed fairly successfully on certain types of carburettors, but it can only be correct on the assumption that engine speed is dependent on the throttle opening, which, as we have seen, is not true in all

A seven-cylinder radial aero engine by Dr. Thomas Fletcher, of Bradford

cases. Increase of load will cause an engine to slow down, though the throttle may be wide open and, conversely, a throttled-down engine may speed up on the release of load.

Most modern carburettors are suction-compensated, though mechanical compensation is still popular on motor-cycles in conjunction with semi-compensated jets. The suction of the engine may be used to control the mixture by acting on an automatic air valve or by jets of special design.

The Mixing Valve

One of the oldest devices which gives some measure of automatic compensation is the " mixing valve," which is still used on some modern engines, and the principles of which are incorporated in many more elaborate carburettors. It consists essentially of an air valve, loaded either by gravity or a light

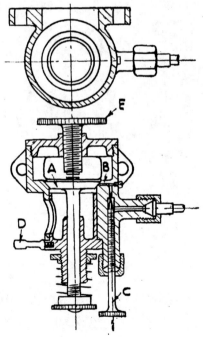

Fig. 42.—Mixing valve as used on " Atom I "

spring, which is opened by the passage of the air to the engine, and the opening of which is utilised in some way to control the discharge of fuel from the jet. It can be used either with or without a float chamber, the latter being more common, and one of its simplest forms is illustrated in Fig. 42. In this device, the fuel jet is situated in the seating of the air valve, and may be either a simple calibrated orifice, or controlled by a needle valve, as shown.

When the engine is not working, the air valve is closed, and also seals off the fuel jet, so that fuel fed to it by gravity cannot flow to waste. Under running conditions, the valve is lifted by suction to the extent required to admit air to the engine, and the passage through the seating of the valve forms the equivalent of a choke tube, through which the air rushes at high velocity. The faster the engine runs, the higher the valve lifts, thus extra air is admitted without increasing the discharge of fuel from the jet. At the slowest engine speeds, the air velocity past the jet is always high enough to ensure good atomisation of the fuel.

The mixing valve used on the 15 c.c. "Atom Minor" engine

The compensation produced by this simple device is not perfect, but one of its virtues is that it assists the engine to make a quick recovery after the speed has been reduced by loading, so that in many cases it may prevent an engine stalling or " conking out." It may be fitted with any form of throttle valve to control engine speed, but sometimes this function is performed by a stop screw over the valve to limit its lift. This, however, affects the compensation if used as a speed control, but is a useful feature when fitted *additional* to the throttle, to check bouncing of the valve at high speed.

Constant-Suction Carburettors

The principles of the mixing valve are employed in some form or other in all carburettors of this type. To improve the accuracy of compensation, the automatic air valve is often used to control a modulating needle in the jet orifice. The best-known carburettor of this type is the S.U., which has

Components of " Atom Minor " mixing valve

The carburettor for the " 1831 " engine

been popular for very many years on motor cars, in which the suction acts on a piston which controls both the air and fuel discharge passages. For simplicity of operating principles, this carburettor is unique, and it has been successfully employed on model petrol engines, but to be successful it demands precise workmanship, particularly in the shaping of the fuel needle, to control the minute quantities of fuel which have to be dealt with.

A simplified automatic carburettor, in which an extra air valve is used to correct the errors of a plain form of carburettor, is illustrated in Fig. 43. This was designed specially for the 30-c.c. engine of the locomotive " 1831 " and has proved capable of coping with a very wide range of engine speed. The spring-loaded air sleeve is damped by air cushioned above it, so that it is free from violent fluctuation which might make the mixture strength erratic.

The Submerged Jet

It has already been seen that the discharge of the jet is affected by the " head " or level of the fuel in the tank or float chamber. If the jet orifice is situated below the fuel level, the tendency of the mixture to weaken as engine speed falls is reduced. A plain jet, situated below the fuel level, would, however, be unsatisfactory, as it would overflow when the engine stopped. The submerged jet must therefore be fitted at the bottom of a jet well, which can fill up above the jet orifice, but cannot overflow while the float feed is working normally. Communication between the jet well and the carburettor air passage is generally made by way of a reduced passage known as a diffuser, the object of which is to improve atomisation and modify the effect of suction on the actual jet, so as to control the degree of compensation.

In many submerged jet carburettors, the jet well and diffuser form what is practically a U-tube, in which the fuel level rises in one leg and sinks in the other as the engine suction increases with the speed. At a certain point or points,

air is admitted to the jet well, and serves the purpose not only
of improving atomisation of fuel, but also diluting the mixture
at high speed, or rather preventing it from becoming too rich.
The " air bleed," as it is called, may be controllable by a screw
valve or fixed by a calibrated orifice. In large carburettors,
one or more submerged jets may be used in conjunction with
plain jets (a well-known example is found in the Zenith carburettor), but simplicity demands that the number of jets
should be kept to the minimum in model carburettors.

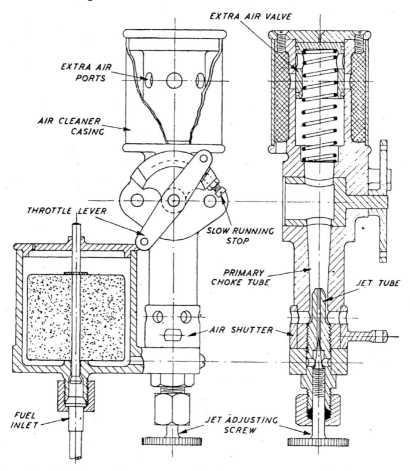

Fig. 43.—General arrangement of carburettor for " 1831 " engine

When the speed of the air through the main choke tube
becomes too low for good atomisation, no system of jet compensation can work really effectively, and thus nearly all
carburettors working on this principle embody a " bypass "or
slow-running jet, which is brought into action by the closing
of the throttle, in order to cope with low speed or " idling "
requirements. This addition is not absolutely necessary on
model engines which are not required to run slowly under any
circumstances, but is nearly always an advantage, even in
engines lesigned purely for racing.

A very successful range of model carburettors has been
produced by the writer, in which a simple form of air-bled
submerged main jet is employed, and the diffuser is in the

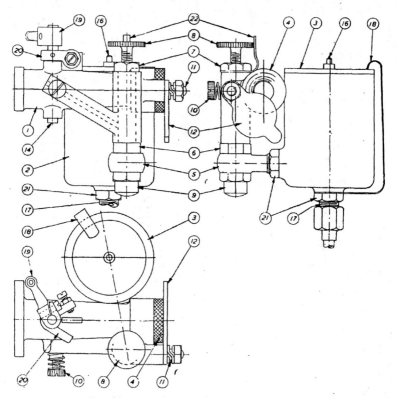

Fig. 44.—The " Atom " type R carburettor

form of an annulus, discharging into the air passage either by a number of small holes, or a narrow slot, extending right round the throat. These are known as the " Atom " carburettors, and the latest of these, known as the Type R, is illustated in Fig. 44.

They embody features which are not yet common in model petrol engine practice, but have been found well worth while when really good carburation and a wide range of automatic control is desired.

Fuel Tanks

The tanks for model petrol engines may be made of very light gauge material so long as joints are soundly made and fittings firmly attached, so as to stand up well to rough use and vibration. Tin or steel tanks are not generally recommended, owing to the liability to internal corrosion which may occur with certain fuels or by the accidental entry of water into tanks. When either pressure feed or bird-feed systems are employed, the tank filler caps should be fitted with fibre washers, so that they can be screwed down quite air-tight, but for other systems, including gravity, suction and pump feed, air vents must be provided. These should not be unnecessarily large, and preferably placed so that foreign matter is not likely to drop into them and clog them, or gain

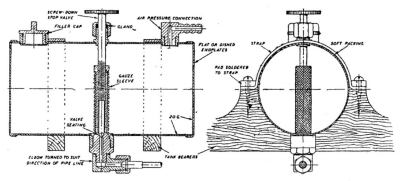

Fig. 45.—Fuel tank with internal stop valve and filter, for use with pressure feed

entry to the tank. Feed pipes should be placed so that they are capable of using nearly all the contents of the tank and not likely to become high and try by any tilting of the tank liable to occur under running conditions. The best place for a fuel filter is inside the tank, where it can be made of ample size and is continually washed clean, but this calls for frequent inspection of the contents of the tank and removal of any collected matter. Pipes must be carefully arranged to prevent air locks, and should have a sufficient degree of flexibility to avoid risk of breakage. Rubber fuel-pipe connections are not advised unless special petrol-resisting rubber is used.

Air Cleaners

These are rarely fitted on model petrol engines, but may, in some cases, be of real practical advantage, and here again, the principles employed in full-size practice are applicable. In the case of model cars running on concrete or dirt tracks, there is more than a probability of picking up abrasive dust in large quantities, and taking it into the engine, with destructive effects ; here is undoubtedly a very strong case for the employment of a dust filter on the air intake.

Steel wool may be used as a filtering medium in such a filter, which can thus be made practically a replica of a simple silencer, and preferably just as large. Another very effective and simple air cleaner consists of a length of perforated tubing, enclosed in a sleeve of flannel or similar fabric, with an outer screen or ventilated casing to protect it from dirt, oil, etc. The centrifugal type of cleaner may also be applicable, but no record of it having been used on a small engine is available.

The actual filter surface of the air cleaner should be as large as possible, not less than twenty times the area of the intake, to allow for partial clogging, and to avoid the need for excessive suction in drawing air through it. Some readjustment of the jet setting may be required after fitting an air cleaner, but if the above precautions are observed, no perceptible reduction of engine power need be involved. Care must be taken to avoid flooding the filter surface with petrol, which may upset carburation, and is liable to increase the risk of a fire at the air intake.

A 30 c.c. Aspin rotary valve engine with Amal type carburettor and built-in magneto, by Mr. N. Boero (see page 208)

CHAPTER IX

IGNITION

ALL model petrol engines now in use employ electric ignition, which is generally provided by means of a battery and coil, but successful high-tension magnetos have now been produced in sizes small enough for all but the very tiniest engines and are likely to become increasingly popular, on account of their obvious advantages in making the engine independent of any separate source of electric power.

To produce a spark capable of bridging the gap of a sparking plug requires a voltage of several thousand volts, the exact voltage depending upon several factors, including the type of sparking plug used and the adjustment of the spark gap. Miniature plugs, specially designed for model petrol engines, will work on lower voltages than full-sized plugs, but still require much higher voltage than can be obtained directly from any normal source of electric power. The only way in which the high voltage can be produced from a small battery or generator is by making use of the principles of the "induction coil," which is the term given to a specialised form of step-up transformer used for producing sparks.

The Induction Coil

The current from a small low-voltage battery can be "stepped up" to a sufficiently high voltage to operate the sparking plug by means of an induction coil. The form of coil used for ignition is essentially similar to the Ruhmkorff coil formerly employed for wireless spark transmission and X-ray apparatus, but adapted in a small and compact form for this particular purpose. It is not practicable within the scope of this book to deal in detail with the electrical theory and design of ignition coils, but it may be mentioned that they usually comprise a soft iron laminated or wire core, on which is wound a primary winding consisting of about 150 turns of fairly heavy wire, and a secondary winding consisting of about 15,000 turns of very fine wire. The primary circuit is energised by the battery and produces a powerful magnetic field in and around the core. When the primary current is interrupted, the magnetic field suddenly collapses, thereby producing an inductive current of very high voltage in the secondary. The ignition coil may thus be described quite correctly as a form of transformer, but its design and function differ in many important respects from that of the ordinary alternating current transformer. Various sizes of ignition coils are used on model engines and, for model aircraft work, successful coils as light as 2 ozs. in weight have been developed. It is obviously more difficult to make efficient small coils than large ones if they are to produce an effective spark, and the difficulty of winding the required number of turns in the available space and of keeping them properly insulated imposes a practical limit in this respect.

A condenser is fitted across the break of an ignition coil to absorb the self-inductive current of the primary, which tends to retard the breakdown of the magnetic field and thereby reduce the efficiency of the secondary. The capacity of this condenser varies according to the size and design of the coil, but values of from 0.1 to 0.5 microfarad are used with small coils, and almost any good quality condenser of approximately the correct capacity will suit this purpose. Metal-cased condensers of a type specially designed for ignition are, however, desirable in engines which work under arduous conditions or where resistance to oil, damp, or vibration are important considerations.

K

Trembler Coils

In the early days of internal combustion engines, coils were commonly fitted with an electro-magnetic contact breaker, working on the same principle as the vibrator of an electric bell or buzzer. This was usually operated by the magnetism of the core, and thus served to break the primary circuit of the coil at the moment the current reached its maximum value, this action being repeated continuously all the time the coil was in circuit with the battery. The result was to produce a continuous stream of sparks at the plug, which was once thought to be more effective for producing ignition than the single discharge produced by the use of a mechanical breaker. A form of rotary switch, or " wipe contact," was fitted to the timing shaft of the engine to control the timing of the stream of sparks, so that it occurred at the correct point of the cycle to enable the engine to work efficiently, means being provided for advancing or retarding the timing to a limited extent.

Although trembler coils have been found unsuitable for use on modern high-speed engines, because of the difficulty of ensuring close precision of timing, they may still be found on some of the older engines or on stationary engines which work at comparatively low r.p.m. The wiring circuit of a trembler coil is extremely simple, as shown in Fig. 46, and the buzz of the trembler when the coil is on contact serves as a proof that it is properly connected, though not necessarily that it is

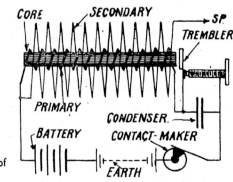

Fig. 46.—Circuit diagram of trembler coil

producing a spark ; but this is just as easy to test out by removing the lead from the plug and holding it—by its insulation, of course—close to any metal part of the engine.

It should be noted that the condenser of a trembler coil is connected across the points of the electro-magnetic contact breaker, and is thus nearly always enclosed in the casing of the coil. If, however, this condenser should become faulty, it is possible to substitute a separate outside condenser for it, after finding and disconnecting the internal wires leading to it. The possibility of taking the breaker out of circuit and using the coil as a non-trembler has also been exploited successfully by several users of model petrol engines. No condenser is required across the wipe contact on the engine, and it should be noted that firing takes place on the completion of the circuit at this point (or rather, a small fraction *after*, depending on several factors, including the adjustment of the trembler spring and the speed of the engine) ; in other words, at the " make."

Non-Trembler Coils

This type of coil is essentially similar to the trembler coil in principle except that the primary circuit is broken by a mechanically-operated breaker fitted to the timing shaft of the engine instead of by an electro-magnetic breaker. Thus

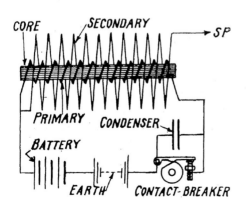

Fig. 47.—Circuit diagram of non-trembler coil

the coil gives only a single spark discharge at each engine cycle, but it is much more accurately timed, as the time lag inseparable from the use of a vibrating spring blade is eliminated. This is important in an engine which runs at several thousand r.p.m. ; for instance, if an engine is running at 3,000 r.p.m., or 50 revolutions per second—which is quite a moderate speed for model petrol engines nowadays—this means that the crank will move 18 degrees in 1/1,000 of a second, so that even so small a time lag will put the timing sufficiently late to impair efficiency very considerably. If the time lag were absolutely constant, it could be compensated by advancing the timing point the required number of degrees at high speed, but in fact it varies from one cycle to another, for various reasons, such as " heterodyning " action of the trembler spring, which tends to act as a reed, with a natural frequency not necessarily in harmony with the magnetism of the core at the moment contact is made.

It should thus be quite clear why the non-trembler coil has completely superseded its older rival for all high-speed engines, quite apart from its greater simplicity and compactness of construction. In most cases a simple cylindrical casing, fitting

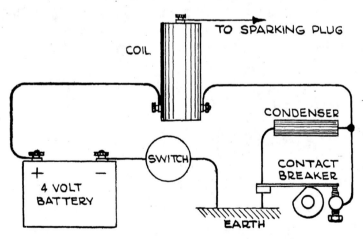

Fig. 48.—Coil ignition wiring diagram, applicable to all small single-cylinder engines

closely over the coil windings, suffices to house the coil, the condenser being usually entirely separate and situated as closely as possible to the mechanical breaker. Thus the bulk and weight of the coil can be kept down to the minimum, an important advantage when the power/weight ratio of the complete engine must be high and space. for its installation is restricted.

The connections for a non-trembler coil are shown in Fig. 47, and it should be noted that the spark occurs at the point when contact is interrupted by the mechanical breaker ; in other words, at the " break." Duration of contact is determined by the " dwell " of the cam which operates the breaker points, and thus the actual period of time during which current flows through the coil becomes shorter as the engine speed increases. As the resistance and impedance of the primary circuit retards the " build-up " of current, a certain minimum time is required to obtain maximum magnetisation of the core prior to the break ; and if less than this is allowed,

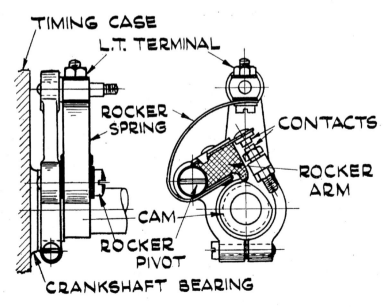

Fig. 49.—Contact breaker for " 1831 " engine, using Lucas type rocker arm

the spark efficiency will be reduced. Thus a high-speed engine will require a longer *angular* period of contact than a slow-speed engine, and in practice nearly all coil ignition systems tend to fall off in spark efficiency at very high engine speeds ; in some cases this constitutes a definite limiting factor to the use of coil ignition.

Contact Breakers

The simple wipe contact used with the trembler coil is not highly satisfactory when used to control a non-trembler coil, and, in actual practice, a more positive and clean-cut means of making and breaking the circuit is universally employed, embodying point contacts which are in turn brought together and separated by the action of a cam.

In most modern contact breakers one of the contacts is stationary, the other being attached either to the blade of a spring or to a pivoted, spring-loaded lever, so that it is normally pressed firmly against its counterpart. A rotating cam, having its surface suitably shaped to produce the required periods of

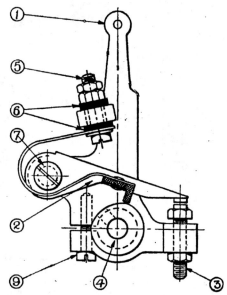

Fig. 50.—Contact-breaker employing a Delco-Remy lightweight interrupter arm. (1) backplate, (2) interrupter arm, (3) contact screw, (4) cam, (5) terminal, (6) insulating bushes, (7) pivot screw, (9) clamping screw

" make " and " break," operates the moving contact, either directly or indirectly, against the action of the loading spring. In some of the early contact breakers, the points were pressed together by means of the cam and allowed to spring apart when released ; modern breakers generally reverse this procedure, as this tends to a more simple and straightforward construction, and the speed of the break can be varied by the design of cam, instead of being controlled by a spring which may possibly alter its tension. Some examples of breakers following the older principles have, however, made their appearance in recent years and are claimed to have certain advantages over the more usual type. Much depends on exact details of design, however, and, generally speaking, either type can be made to give perfectly satisfactory results.

The cams employed in contact-breakers are usually of the disc type, having the working contour on their periphery, but face cams have also been used and are quite satisfactory provided that they have a fixed endwise location ; but if the shafts to which they are attached have any end float, this may possibly cause a variation of the timing sufficient to affect engine efficiency. In most cases the cam is attached to a shaft

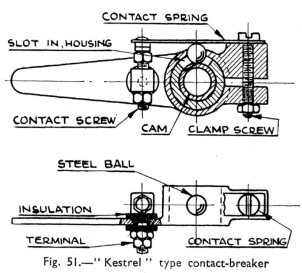

Fig. 51.—" Kestrel " type contact-breaker

which rotates once per cycle of the engine, i.e. the main shaft of a two-stroke, or the camshaft of a four-stroke, and thus, in a single-cylinder engine of either type, a single-break cam is employed. Multi-cylinder engines may have a single coil serving all the cylinders, in which case the cam has as many breaks as there are cylinders; in this case a high-tension distributor is used to distribute the spark to each of the cylinders in turn. Sometimes, however, engines are fitted with separate coils for each cylinder, in which case a pair of contact points is required for each coil; these are spaced around the timing shaft at intervals corresponding to the firing sequence of the cylinders, and operated in turn by a single-break cam.

The design of the cam has an important bearing not only on the sharpness of the break, but also on the effort required to drive it and the speed at which the breaker will work efficiently. A very abrupt break may be mechanically inefficient and tend to cause the interrupter lever to bounce. In many small model petrol engines a very crude type of cam, consisting simply of a disc with a flat filed on it, has been

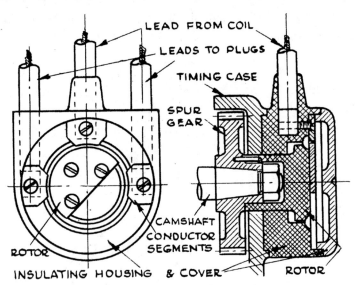

Fig. 52.—High-tension distribution as used on "1831" engine

employed ; but it can be demonstrated that friction can be considerably reduced, and mechanical action much improved, by careful attention to the cam design. Other factors which influence the action of the contact breaker are the inertia of the lever or spring blade, which should be kept as low as possible, consistent with necessary strength and rigidity, and the strength of the loading spring, which must be heavy enough to ensure firm contact, but not excessively heavy so as to cause unnecessary friction.

A simple form of spring blade contact breaker which has few working parts and is well suited for use on small light-weight engines is illustrated in Fig. 51. For engines which are intended to run at very high speed, the contact breakers illustrated in Figs. 49 and 50 are considered more suitable. These have pivoted rockers, in one case built up of sheet steel

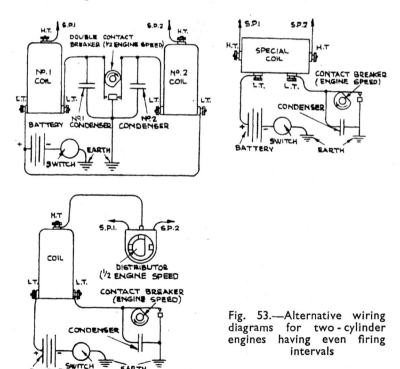

Fig. 53.—Alternative wiring diagrams for two - cylinder engines having even firing intervals

with a fibre pad and bush attached, in the other consisting almost entirely of a solid fibre block.

The contact points must be made of a metal which is not liable to pit or oxydise by the spark which occurs at the break. In full-size practice, tungsten-tipped contacts are almost universally employed nowadays, and these answer quite well for model engines if a condenser of the correct value is used. The platinum-iridium contacts formerly used in the old coil or magneto-ignition systems do not stand up so long to heavy wear, and have the further disadvantage of being very expensive, but they are less liable to increase their contact resistance through the film of oil which finds its way into nearly all small breakers. Other contact metals may be regarded as unsuitable for use in ignition apparatus, with the possible exception of silver or silver-gold alloy, which have been successfully used in a few cases.

One mistake sometimes made by designers of very small engines is to attempt to make the contact-breaker mechanism to scale size. While, theoretically, a very tiny breaker should be capable of performing its function effectively, it may be too delicate to stand up to arduous conditions of running, and contact adjustment is liable to be finicky and difficult of access.

High-Tension Magnetos

Apart from the obvious advantage of dispensing with the need for a battery, the magneto appeals to the progressive model petrol engine constructor as a more suitable ignition system for a self-contained high-efficiency power plant. A good magneto is also much less liable to impose any limitation on engine speed than the best battery and coil system, though it is possibly at some disadvantage at the other end of the range, i.e. at starting or very low speed. The magneto, in generating its power mechanically, is bound to absorb some power from the engine, but this is less than is commonly believed or estimated.

On the larger sizes of model engines, it is sometimes possible to use a standard type of magneto, though both the size and weight are greater than is desirable. Adaptation of an existing magneto by cutting it down to a skeleton or incorporating its essential working parts in a special lightweight body, or into the engine design, is also possible, but there are obvious limitations in such a scheme, and the best examples of this form of ignition on model engines are found in specially designed and constructed magnetos.

Twin two-stroke engine, showing high-tension distributor mounted on crankshaft

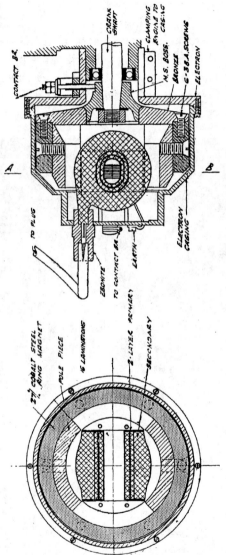

Fig. 54.—The Rankine flywheel magneto, suitable for model racing engines from 15 to 30 c.c.

Perhaps the best-known, and certainly one of the most successful, of these magnetos is that designed and used by Mr. A. D. Rankine in his racing speed boats. It is of the flywheel type, having a rotary ring magnet mounted on a bronze disc, which takes the place of the normal engine flywheel, and a stationary armature, which is identical in shape and winding specification with the armature of a standard motor-cycle magneto. This is a very attractive feature, as it simplifies the construction by removing the necessity for a delicate winding operation.

Another pioneer flywheel magneto, which has been working successfully since it was first constructed twenty years ago, is the original " Atom " magneto, illustrated in Fig. 55.

This bears a general resemblance to the well-known Villiers flywheel magneto, having a two-pole ring magnet built into the rim of a bronze flywheel and an offset magnet coil with laminated pole pieces attached to the ends mounted on a stationary backplate. The diameter of this magneto is greater than is generally convenient for use on a model engine in cases where space is restricted, and the extent to which it can be reduced in diameter is limited by the practicable size of magnet coil, but it is a highly efficient spark generator and, from the point of view of adaptability to existing engines, has much to commend it. As the main shaft can extend beyond the flywheel, it can be fitted in an accessible position at the front of a model aircraft engine.

It is only within recent years that magnetos sufficiently small to conform to the scale of the more popular sizes of model petrol engines have been developed. This has been made possible partly by taking advantage of the qualities of new and improved magnet steels now available, but even more by patient research in the design of suitable armature coils and other essential components, so as to obtain the maximum electrical efficiency from magnetos of very small dimensions.

One of the most efficient and reliable magnet steels in commercial production consists of an alloy of iron, aluminium,

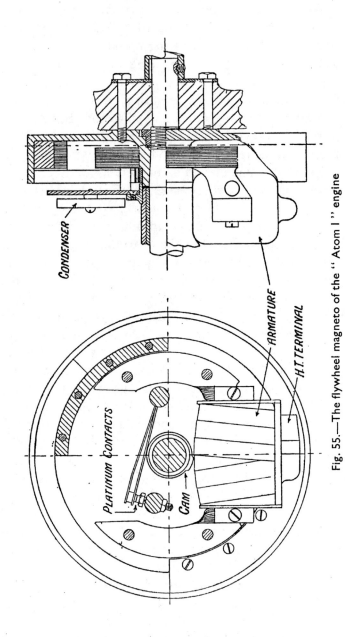

CONDENSER

ARMATURE

H.T. TERMINAL

PLATINUM CONTACTS

CAM

Fig. 55.—The flywheel magneto of the " Atom I " engine

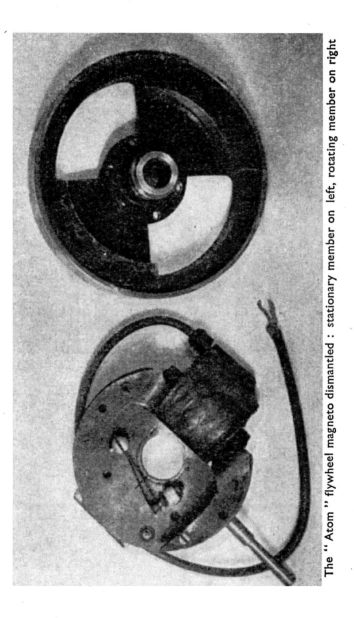

The " Atom " flywheel magneto dismantled : stationary member on left, rotating member on right

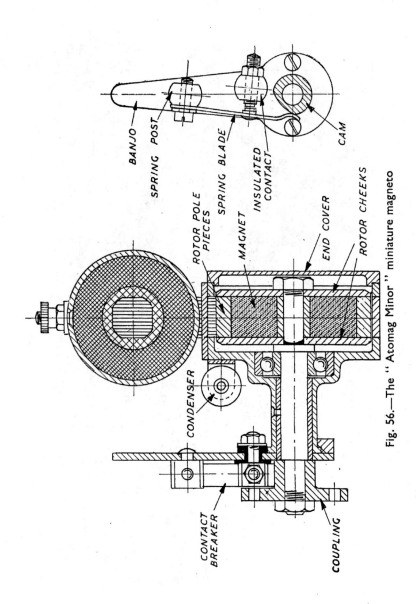

BANJO

SPRING POST

ROTOR POLE PIECES

SPRING BLADE

MAGNET

INSULATED CONTACT

CAM

END COVER

ROTOR CHEEKS

CONDENSER

CONTACT BREAKER

COUPLING

Fig. 56.—The " Atomag Minor " miniature magneto

nickel and cobalt known as Alnico. It has been found possible to make a successful magneto with a disc magnet of this material, a little over 1 in. in diameter and weighing only 2 ozs., to take the place of the bulky horseshoe magnet formerly necessary. The weight of the complete magneto is 8 ozs., and it is thus quite suitable for use on an engine as small as 5 c.c., being no heavier than the coil and battery generally used on such an engine. This magneto is known as the " Atomag Minor," and is shown in Figs. 56 and 57. Although this will work effectively on larger engines, a larger version of the same design, the " Atomag Major " is recommended, more particularly when racing conditions call for an extra margin of spark efficiency.

Another small magneto of interest to model petrol engine constructors is the " Atomax," the unique feature of which is that it is specially designed as a " conversion unit," to take the place of a coil ignition system on existing engines, or those

A completely metal-clad ("screened") example of the " Atomag "

with no provision for the fitting of a magneto. This device, illustrated below, is a true flywheel magneto, as the rotary magnet is sufficiently large and massive to take the place of the engine flywheel, but the stationary coil and pole pieces, unlike those of most flywheel magnetos, are situated outside the radius of the flywheel. To convert a normal engine to magneto ignition, it is only necessary to substitute the rotary magnet for the ordinary flywheel and bolt the stator frame to the engine bearers, or otherwise attach it to the engine, so that the pole pieces just clear the magnet poles by about 0.005 in. The original contact breaker and condenser fitted to the engine can be used simply by connecting them in circuit with the primary of the magneto armature. As the magnet has four poles, it completes its electrical cycle in half the angular distance of the ordinary two-pole magnet, which is equivalent to doubling the speed, so that the efficiency of the spark at low engine speed is correspondingly increased and starting thereby facilitated.

Components for the " Atomax " conversion unit

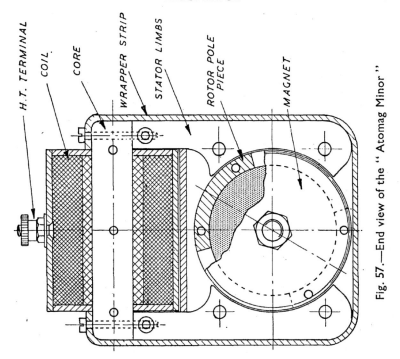

Fig. 57.—End view of the "Atomag Minor"

All the magnetos described above are of the rotary magnet type, which is in keeping with the latest full-size practice, and not only conducive to the most efficient use of modern magnet steels, but also to the simplest mechanical design and construction. The more orthodox rotary armature magnetos, and also polar inductor types, have also been successfully made in a fairly small size but, generally speaking, involve far more difficulty and complication in construction.

To those readers who are not conversant with the modern rotary magnet magneto, whether of the flywheel type or otherwise, it may be remarked that its electrical working principles are identical with those of the older magneto except that the roles of the fixed and moving components are reversed. This simplifies the design and eliminates the need for slip rings or other rubbing contacts, but is only practicable when a small compact magnet, preferably approximating to a disc or

ring in shape, can be used. Polar inductor magnetos work
without relative movement of either the magnet or the
armature coil, the moving member being a system of soft iron
pole shoes or " inductors " which convey the magnetic flux
in alternating order from the magnet poles to the extremities
of the iron core passing through the coil.

Sparking Plugs

In the early days of model petrol engines, the only sparking
plugs commercially produced were the 18-mm. De Dion
standard type used in full-size practice, which were manifestly
very much out of scale for models, especially those of small
capacity, and in many cases seriously restricted the development of design. Several attempts were made to manufacture
miniature plugs on a small scale, but the first reliable plugs
available of a more or less suitable size were the 12-mm.
type, originally manufactured for use on light aircraft engines.
These were produced by a number of well-known firms,
including K.L.G., Lodge and Bosch, so that a range of plugs
of varying characteristics were available to suit various types
of engines. The 12-mm. plug is still extensively used for
racing engines in the 30-c.c. and 15-c.c. classes, but it is on the
large side for engines smaller than this.

The next miniature plug to arrive was the $\frac{3}{8}$-in., and this,
being specially designed for model engines, was quite suitable
for much smaller engines. At a later date the $\frac{1}{4}$-in. plug was
introduced, and this is by no means out of scale proportion to
an engine of only 1 c.c., so that it may be said that ready-made
plugs are now available for all sizes of engines within the scope
of this book.

It should, however, be noted that the $\frac{3}{8}$-in. and $\frac{1}{4}$-in. plugs
are primarily intended to suit the requirements of commercially-made model engines, almost invariably of the two-stroke
type, and working on a concentrated " petroil " mixture. The
main characteristic of these plugs is resistance to over-oiling,
to obtain which the insulators are designed to retard too rapid

cooling, and the electrodes are finely pointed, with the same end in view. Such plugs give excellent results on the majority of model engines, but may be found unsuitable for racing engines, working at high compression and dealing with a greater quantity or intensity of heat. In such cases heavier electrodes and more efficiently cooled insulators are desirable to prevent overheating and pre-ignition, but so far as is known at the time of writing, plugs having these features are not obtainable in sizes smaller than 12 mm.

It may be mentioned that a plug designed for use in a fairly cool or oily engine is generally known as a " soft " plug, and one for a high-compression " hot" engine as a " hard " plug. An engine of the latter type, if fitted with too soft a plug, will often knock badly after it has been running for some time, and not infrequently continues to run—somewhat inefficiently —after the ignition is switched off. This symptom indicates that the plug electrodes have become incandescent and are capable of igniting the mixture before the correct time, hence the term " pre-ignition." Too hard a plug, on the other hand, may cause the engine to misfire badly, or even to cut out altogether, through oil or petrol vapour condensing on the electrodes. Sometimes it is found necessary to start a racing engine on a soft or medium plug and change it for a hard one after the engine has warmed up, but generally it is possible to find a plug having a range of heat tolerance wide enough to cover all conditions of running in a particular engine. It is a sound rule not to use a harder plug than is found really necessary ; some users imagine that a hard plug assists them to obtain a high engine performance, but it is more likely to increase their difficulties, and should be used only when it can be proved to have a beneficial effect. No definite rule can be laid down as to what type of plug is required for a specific type of engine or standard of performance, owing to the way engines vary in heat tolerance or oil control.

Many users of model petrol engines have found it necessary to make their own sparking plugs, owing to the difficulty of obtaining a plug of suitable characteristics for their particular engine. Indeed, sometimes miniature plugs of any kind have been impossible to obtain. The most difficult part of the plug to produce, from the amateur's point of view, is the insulator, and various insulating materials have been used with varying degrees of success. A common expedient is to grind down the insulator of a larger plug, but insulators of steatite, mica, glass and quartz have also been found satisfactory. Within recent years, a new refractory insulating material known as Mycalex has been produced. This is a compound of powdered mica and fused glass, which can either be moulded or machined to shape. Satisfactory plugs, down to the very smallest sizes, have been produced by many amateurs with the aid of this material, and even when ready-made plugs are available the facility which it offers for developing a plug of special design for a particular purpose is a valuable advantage.

In some cases the normal type of sparking plug takes up much more room in the cylinder head of a small engine than can conveniently be spared, and it may be found expedient to dispense with the usual plug body by fitting the insulator to a gland in the cylinder head itself. The spark gap in such plugs is usually annular, and formed by a small concentric hole which gives the required clearance around the central electrode ; but, if desired, a bar or other form of side electrode can be fitted inside the head. One disadvantage of this form of plug constiuction is that it necessitates removal of the cylinder head to check the spark gap or to ascertain by visual observation whether the plug is sparking.

Cleaning and reconditioning is occasionally necessary for miniature plugs, as with the full-sized type, but is much more difficult, owing to the small cavity and the fine clearance around the insulator. Sand-blasting, by the use of apparatus similar to that used in service stations for full-sized plugs, is the most effective method of removing carbon and semi-burnt oil, but the abrasive powder used must be very fine, and the greatest care taken to remove all traces of it after use. A detachable insulator is a great advantage in this respect, but rarely obtainable in commercially-made miniature plugs ; it is somewhat difficult to ensure that such insulators are properly gastight, and their delicate construction makes it necessary to exercise the greatest care in screwing down the retaining gland.

Examples of sparking plugs in 14 mm., 12 mm., $\frac{3}{8}$ in. and $\frac{1}{4}$ in. standard sizes

CHAPTER X

LUBRICATION AND COOLING

THE various systems of lubrication employed in full-size practice are all capable of being adapted successfully for use on model engines, though the latter are often very poorly equipped in this respect and are expected to work well with the most haphazard and primitive methods of lubrication. It is true that in some respects the model engine is easier to lubricate, as it is rarely expected to run continuously for very long periods, and economy of oil consumption is of little or no importance ; but it is none the less true that small engines, no less than large ones, run all the more smoothly and efficiently when properly lubricated, and also keep in sound and reliable working order for much longer periods than when " hit-and-miss " methods of lubrication are employed.

The " Petroil " System

The great majority of two-stroke engines, at least in the smaller sizes, employ an extremely simple but none the less reliable system of lubrication, which consists of mixing a certain proportion of oil with the fuel. This is fed to the carburettor and sprayed from the jet, always in the same proportion as the fuel but, being much less volatile, it deposits out from the fuel more or less completely in its passage through the engine. As the fuel mixture passes through the crankcase in the normal two-stroke engine, the oil which deposits out settles on the working parts and keeps them lubricated. The proportion of oil in the fuel varies according to the type, size and speed of the engine and, generally speaking, the smaller the engine, the higher the concentration of oil required. A 250-c.c. motor-cycle engine may run quite satisfactorily on a mixture of 1 part oil to 16 parts of petrol, while a 5-c.c. engine may require 1 part oil to 4 parts of petrol ; the most suitable proportions must be found by trial, and represent a compromise between under-oiling, with excessive friction and heavy wear on the one hand, and over-oiling, which causes fouling of the sparking plugs and an excessively smoky exhaust, on the other.

Although the oil supplied in this way is in proportion to the fuel used, it is not necessarily in proportion to the load, consequently engines thus lubricated are liable to smoke on light load and " starve " on heavy load. As the oil is left to find its way into the bearings by capillary attraction, and is not positively fed to the places where it is most required, it cannot cope so effectively with the requirements of heavy

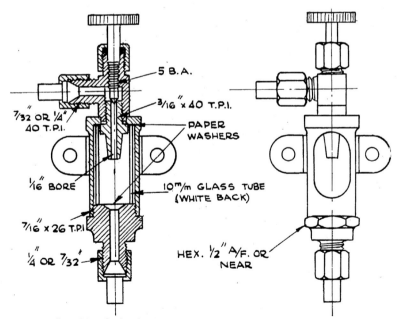

Fig. 58.—Sight feed lubricator, in section and elevation

duty as a positive feed system. Some of the oil sprayed into the engine does not deposit out—especially when the engine is hot—and is thus carried to waste in the exhaust gas, a fact which often gives the two-stroke engine a bad reputation, as it is liable to cover surfaces which happen to be in line with the exhaust ports with a film of sooty oil.

Notwithstanding these limitations, the petroil system gives highly satisfactory results on small engines, but for the highest speed and performance, the addition of a positive pressure feed to the most heavily-loaded bearings is an advantage. This also allows the proportion of the oil in the fuel to be reduced, which facilitates fine control of the carburettor jet adjustment (as the viscosity of the fuel is reduced) and reduces the liability to foul the sparking plug.

Positive Feed Systems

The normal type of four-stroke engine cannot be lubricated by the petroil system, as the mixture does not come into contact with the crankshaft bearings, though a small amount of oil is sometimes mixed with the fuel to improve " upper " lubrication (i.e. cylinder and valves). Some types of four-stroke

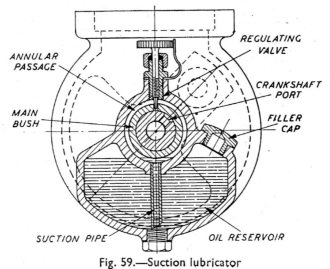

ANNULAR PASSAGE

REGULATING VALVE

CRANKSHAFT PORT

MAIN BUSH

FILLER CAP

SUCTION PIPE

OIL RESERVOIR

Fig. 59.—Suction lubricator

engines have been devised in which the mixture passes through the crankcase, but these have disadvantages in other respects and are not highly popular. One method which was formerly popular in these engines is the so-called " splash " system, which consisted simply of pouring or pumping a certain quantity of oil into a closed crankcase and allowing it to be churned round by the working parts. This cannot, however, be regarded as a satisfactory method for a high-speed engine, as the oil sets up friction or " oil drag," and the amount in effective use at any particular time is indeterminate, particularly when the amount and frequency of the dose are not accurately measured.

Continuous oiling, by feeding regulated quantities of oil direct to the bearings, is much to be preferred. The simplest method of effecting this is by the " drip-feed " lubricator, such as used extensively on stationary engines. The device used for this purpose is commonly equipped with a sight glass and a fine adjustment valve with means of cutting off the supply.

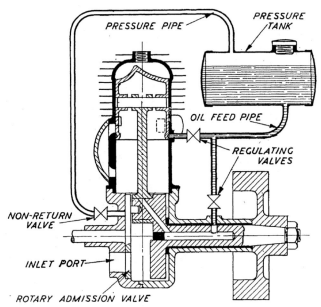

Fig. 60.—Crankcase pressure lubrication system

Pressure and Suction Systems

Something better than gravity is very desirable to ensure the reliable feeding of viscous oils, and a convenient method of forcing the oil is to make use of crankcase pressure, obtained by the displacement of the piston in single-cylinder engines. In four-stroke engines it is usual to release the pressure on the down-stroke of the piston by means of a non-return valve ; the suction on the up-stroke can then be utilised to draw oil from a small supply tank through a control valve. This system is fully automatic, as the suction does not continue after the engine stops, and has been found to work reliably on engines such as the " Kiwi."

Two-stroke engines will also draw oil into the bearings in this way, and the effective pressure may be considerably increased if the oil tank is made airtight, and pressure from the crankcase communicated to it on the down-stroke of the piston through a small non-return valve, as in Fig. 60.

A method of lubrication which has been used extensively for racing engines, both four-stroke and two-stroke, in the

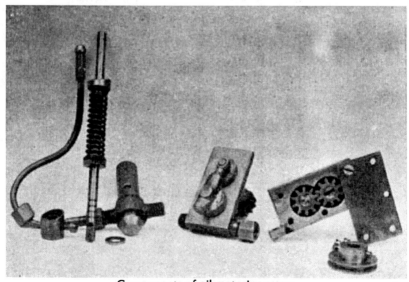

Components of oil metering pump

past, is to make the oil reservoir in the form of a pump or syringe with a spring-loaded plunger, which forces the oil through a control valve to the engine bearings. Some form of catch is usually provided to hold the plunger back and prevent it from feeding oil when the engine is stopped.

Engine-driven pumps are sometimes employed to effect the same purpose, and have important practical advantages, especially if means are provided for varying the output to suit the needs of the engine. The most suitable type of pump for this particular duty is a small plunger pump working at a low speed. Ratchet gear similar to that used for mechanical oil pumps on locomotives is sometimes employed on petrol engines, but single or compound worm gearing is more compact and efficient. Oscillating or other valveless pumps are conducive to reliability, as small valves often stick or leak, however carefully fitted.

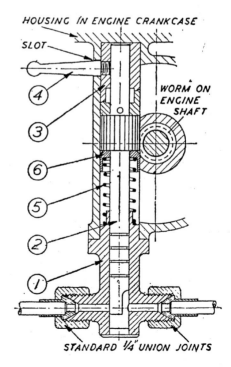

HOUSING IN ENGINE CRANKCASE

SLOT

WORM ON ENGINE SHAFT

④
③
⑥
⑤
②
①

STANDARD ¼" UNION JOINTS

Fig. 61.—Metering oil pump, suitable for engines up to 30 c.c.

A variable-output metering pump which has been used successfully on several types of engines is illustrated on page 162. This has a plunger which rotates and reciprocates simultaneously, and the end of which acts as a rotary valve to control suction and discharge ports. Control of output is effected by turning the cam which imparts reciprocating motion to the plunger, so that any required proportion of the stroke can be rendered ineffective when the full displacement of the pump is not required. (See also Figs. 61 and 62.)

Oil Circulation Systems

The methods of oil feeding so far described have all been " total-loss" or metering systems, in which a small quantity of oil is fed to the engine and no attempt is made to recover any part of it after use. Modern four-stroke engines, however, often have an oil circulation system, in which comparatively large quantities of oil are flushed through the bearings, drained or pumped into a sump or reserve tank and again drawn upon by the pump for further use. This system is not

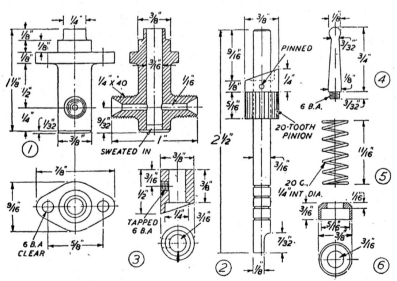

Fig. 62.—Details of oil metering pump

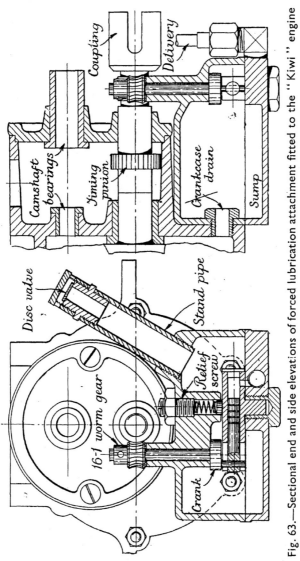

Fig. 63.—Sectional end and side elevations of forced lubrication attachment fitted to the "Kiwi" engine

necessarily more economical of oil, but it enables the oil to be
used as a coolant as well as a lubricant, so that the bearings
can be loaded more heavily without risk of failure.

Metering control of the pump output is in this case unnecessary, but sometimes it is found desirable to fit a relief valve
to release excess oil pressure and avoid overloading the pump.
A simple system of this type is fitted to the " Kittiwake "
engine, an oscillating type of pump being used, driven from a
vertical crankshaft worm-geared from the main engine shaft

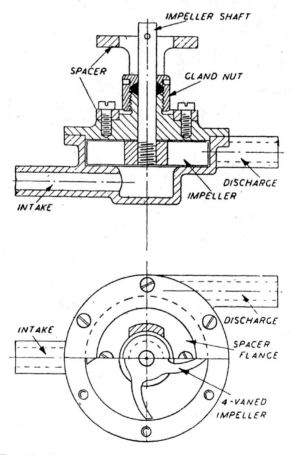

Fig. 64.—Vertical shaft circulating pump as used on the
" Wall " multi-cylinder engine

at a ratio of 16 to 1. The twin-cylinder engine of the loco-motive " 1831 " has a small gearwheel pump running at half engine speed.

The sump should always be isolated to some extent from the main crankcase to allow the oil to settle, undisturbed by the agitation of the working parts. A simple gravity sump is recommended on the grounds of simplicity and reliability, as the use of a scavenge oil pump not only adds complication, but may also be less reliable when dealing with frothy oil.

It is quite possible to circulate oil without using a pump, and this method is recommended for engines which are not required for very heavy duty. This can be done by isolating a part of the crankcase in the form of a trough under the big-end bearing, which may be fitted with a dipper or impact feed scoop. A small oil hole in the bottom of the trough (its size may be calibrated by trial, but is not at all critical) allows oil to seep upwards from the main sump to continually replace that displaced by the connecting rod. The normal oil level must, of course, be high enough to cause the oil to flow by gravity, but not to overflow over the top of the trough.

Lubricating Oils

The quality of oil used for model engines is just as important as that used in full-size practice and, generally speaking, the

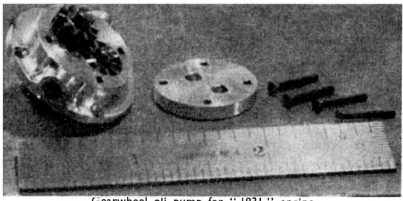

Gearwheel oil pump for " 1831 " engine

same grades of oil can be used for corresponding classes of duty. Fairly viscous oils are necessary in most cases, but it is a mistake to assume that the heaviest oils are the most efficient lubricants or resist heat most effectively. For petroil lubrication, an oil which can be held in suspension in the fuel is essential ; this applies to nearly all mineral oils, but not to special vegetable-base racing oils. The latter are, however, soluble in alcohol and certain other blended fuels. Vegetable oils are not considered so indispensable for racing nowadays as they used to be, however, and have certain practical disadvantages which make it undesirable to use them unless it is found absolutely necessary.

Cooling

Examples of both water-cooled and air-cooled engines are found in model practice, the latter being far the more popular at the present time by reason of their greater simplicity. Effective air cooling presents no difficulty in the case of model aircraft engines, which run in a powerful air current created by the propeller, and speed-boat engines, though somewhat less favourably placed in this respect, are not really difficult to keep cool if well designed. The part of the engine most likely to overheat is the cylinder head, which should always be well finned ; the barrel is less important, especially in a four-stroke engine. Two-stroke engines sometimes have a hot region around the exhaust port, but heat conductivity is always fairly good in small engines, and overheating trouble comparatively rare. Air-cooled engines are capable of working over a wide range of temperature and can be run quite efficiently at almost any temperature below the carbonisation point of the oil so long as distortion of the cylinder can be avoided.

Water-cooling is often used for stationary and marine engines, in conditions where a draught of air is not conveniently available. Most stationary engines have a cooling tank of sufficient capacity to absorb all the heat liable to be generated on the longest run the engine is required to make, and circulation is maintained on the thermo-syphon principle. Marine engines usually take water from outside the hull and force it through the water jacket, finally discharging it overboard or into the exhaust pipe; but in cases where the water is muddy or full of weeds it may be an advantage to use a "closed circuit" system similar to that used for a stationary engine. It is possible to carry away heat very rapidly by water cooling,

A 15 c.c. two-stroke engine by Mr. Ian Bradley, having a water-cooled cylinder head. Note water circulation pump driven by flexible spring coupling

and it may thus be found very desirable for engines developing very high power; but opinions are divided on this subject, and there have been few water-cooled engines used in racing boats of recent years.

Water cooling limits the temperature range within which the engine will work, as water cannot exist in the jackets at a higher temperature than 212° F. ; this applies to the normal circulation system which is in free communication with the atmosphere. To raise the limit of working temperature, the system may be designed to work at a pressure, or a fluid of higher boiling point than water may be used as the coolant. The extra complication of these systems, however, is undesirable in a model engine and, so far as is known, they have not been used to advantage. In systems where fresh, cold water is taken into the jackets, the very small quantity required for effective cooling of a model engine often makes it very difficult to control the temperature between two extremes. The adaptability of water-cooled engines is restricted, and the bulk and weight of the cooling tank and other appurtenances, which must always be fitted up wherever and whenever the engine is run, often constitute an objection to their use.

Where water circulation by the thermo-syphon method is impracticable, some means of forcing water through the jackets is necessary. Pumps of the plunger, gearwheel and centrifugal types may all be adapted to this work, the latter being the simplest of all, and quite reliable if properly arranged, but it is often made several sizes too large for its job. A pump with an impeller 1 in. in diameter is amply large enough to circulate all the water required for cooling a 30-c.c. engine when run at half engine speed. Wherever possible, the pump should be incorporated in the engine design and driven by internal gearing or direct coupled to an available shaft. Extraneous belt-driven pumps may be fairly satisfactory, but never 100 per cent. reliable, and are difficult to install really neatly. A suitable pump for this purpose is shown in Fig. 64.

The circulating pump may be dispensed with in a model

boat by making use of the inertia of the water, as the boat moves forward, to lift water and force it through the jackets, in the same way as a locomotive picks up water from a trough between the tracks. This requires only the fitting of a simple scoop to the bottom of the boat, and has proved entirely satisfactory in all types of boats running at speeds from four or five miles an hour upwards.

An alternative to water cooling in prototype boats or for stationary installations, where no natural draught for air cooling is available, is to equip the engine with a cooling fan to supply a forced draught. This method is becoming increasingly popular, as it enables " general-purpose " air-cooled engines to be adapted to such work with no major structural alteration and the minimum of fittings or attachments. The most suitable fan for this purpose is the enclosed centrifugal type having an air trunk to direct the air to where its effect is most useful, i.e. the parts of the engine most subject to becoming heated. Other types of fans, however, including open propeller fans, have been used successfully.

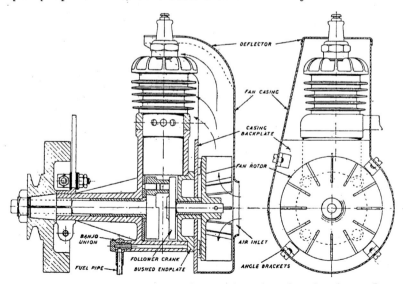

Fig. 65.—An enclosed centrifugal fan for forced cooling fitted to a 5 c.c. " Kestrel " engine

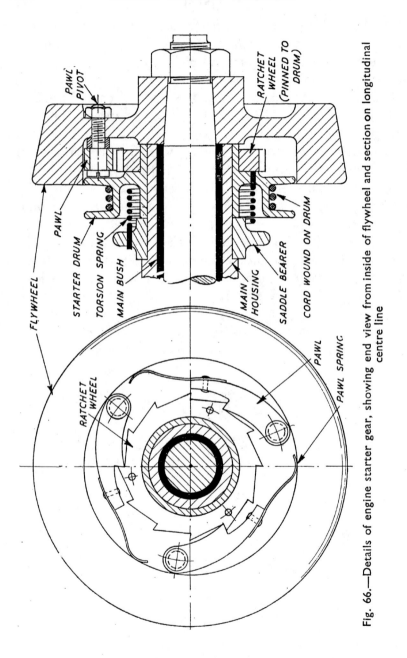

PAWL PIVOT

RATCHET WHEEL (PINNED TO DRUM)

FLYWHEEL

PAWL

STARTER DRUM

TORSION SPRING

MAIN BUSH

MAIN HOUSING

SADDLE BEARER

CORD WOUND ON DRUM

RATCHET WHEEL

PAWL

PAWL SPRING

Fig. 66.—Details of engine starter gear, showing end view from inside of flywheel and section on longitudinal centre line

Starting Gear

Special provision for starting small petrol engines is generally regarded as an unnecessary complication. Marine or stationary engines usually have nothing more than a simple pulley on the shaft, around which a length of cord can be wound to enable the engine to be given a few sharp turns, in the same manner as a spinning top. An alternative method, very popular for starting speed-boat engines, is to make this pulley with a fairly deep vee groove, to receive a round leather or fabric belt, passing only halfway round it and gripping the sides by friction ; both ends of the belt are held, one in each hand, and the engine is spun " *a la diabolo*." Model aircraft engines are generally started by swinging the propeller, but in some cases, aids to starting are found desirable, and these may be operated by hand or any other motive power applied through a claw or free-wheel clutch. Spring-driven starters, capable of storing sufficient energy to turn the engine over several times against compression, are sometimes employed.

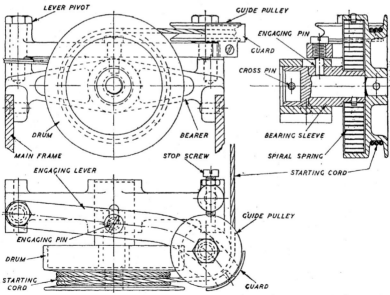

Fig. 67.—General arrangement of self-winding cord starter unit for engine of " 1831 "

The starting pulley may sometimes with advantage be fitted with a ratchet or freewheel to facilitate winding the cord, and a further elaboration of this idea is to make the pulley self-winding by fitting it with a spiral or helical torsion spring. Devices of this type have sometimes fallen into disrepute simply because they were badly designed or executed, so that they either failed to work reliably according to plan or, worse still, jammed solid so as to put the engine completely out of action. A self-winding starter which has proved satisfactory in practice is that illustrated in Fig. 66, which is designed for the " Atom V " engine ; another, equally successful, is that for the engine of the model locomotive " 1831," shown in Fig. 67, which is in the form of a complete unit, separate from the engine and mounted in line with the end of the shaft, which it drives by means of a claw clutch. This starter is adaptable for use with many types of engines.

A 15 c.c. "split-single" supercharged two-stroke engine by Mr. A. D. Rankine (see *page* 201)

CHAPTER XI

RUNNING, MAINTENANCE AND TUNING

WHATEVER type of engine is employed, and to whatever duty it is applied, it is most important that the user should learn to understand its merits and limitations, so that it may be enabled to give its best service under the particular conditions, and kept in good running order with the minimum amount of work. Many constructors will spend a great deal of time building an engine, but grudge the time taken to study its idiosyncrasies and eliminate its curable faults. It is no exaggeration to say that no two engines, even those of apparently identical design, are ever quite alike in their performance, adjustments and temperament—a fact which makes them as interesting to handle as spirited animals—and it is worth while and, indeed, fascinating, to study them carefully under actual running conditions. It does not hurt a good engine to give it plenty of running, so long as it is not abused by racing it without load or neglecting such important services as cooling and lubrication. As far as possible, the engine should be subjected to conditions of normal duty, or at least an attempt should be made to simulate them as closely as possible.

One of the best and quickest ways to get acquainted with an engine is by carefully-conducted bench tests, in which the load, speed and other important factors are closely observed. The subject of bench testing cannot be fully discussed in this book, but its possibilities should never be neglected by users of model petrol engines who are interested in exploiting their possibilities to the utmost, whether in racing or in other ways. The various methods of measuring horse-power in full-size practice are all applicable to model engines, though the

175

simpler types of friction brakes are difficult to manage on engines of high speed and low torque. Fluid friction in some form or other is much more tractable, and special hydraulic and electric dynamometers have been developed for testing model engines. Fan brakes are also extensively used for applying a flexible load to small engines, but are not capable of measuring power directly, though they can be calibrated by running them on an engine of known torque and speed. The power of an engine loaded by means of an uncalibrated fan brake or airscrew or, indeed, by any convenient method of absorbing power may, however, be measured if the engine is mounted on a torque reaction cradle which is capable of moving in a limited arc around the axis of rotation. The torque exerted on the cradle is weighed by means of a spring balance or other means, and the horse-power is then found by the simple formula $\dfrac{W\,2\pi\,R\,N}{33,000}$, where W is the weight balanced, in pounds, R the radius of torque arm in feet, and N the revolutions per minute. This method gives a measurement of power at one torque and speed, but to explore the full range of torque and speed by this method it would be necessary to vary the load, such as by using a fan with variable blades or a range of airscrews of different diameter and pitch. It is much easier to plot a power curve if the load can be varied while the engine is running and, in this respect, a specially designed dynamometer offers the most convenient means of testing.

It is only by knowing exactly what power the engine is capable of producing at any part of the range of speed that one can find how to use its power to full advantage, or be quite certain that any adjustments or modifications, made with a view to improving its performance, are really effective.

Running Attention

Model petrol engines call for much the same kind of attention as larger engines and, if well designed and constructed and used for duties suited to their power and characteristics, should not be any more troublesome. Periodical overhauls and inspection, including decarbonising and cleaning of the parts liable to become fouled, are necessary to keep the engine in running trim, but continual tinkering with it are neither necessary nor desirable. Engines should not be stripped down except for some important purpose, and even when the tuning or development of engines for racing demands constant alteration one should not disturb their internal working parts without urgent reason. Engines often take some time to settle down to smooth and efficient working condition after they have been dismantled.

The greatest care should be taken to avoid foreign matter entering the engine, and this implies making sure that the fuel, oil, water and air which pass through the engine are pure and clean. To make doubly sure that there is no foreign matter in the fuel, a filter funnel should always be used for filling the tank, even though there may be a filter in the pipe line. Oil filters are not usually practicable in a small engine,

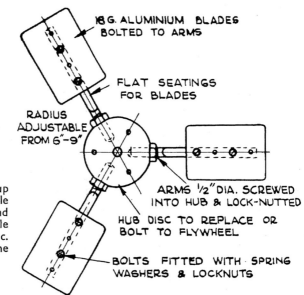

Fig. 68.—A built-up fan brake adjustable for both pitch and diameter, suitable for testing a 30 c.c. high-speed engine

18 G. ALUMINIUM BLADES BOLTED TO ARMS

FLAT SEATINGS FOR BLADES

RADIUS ADJUSTABLE FROM 6″–9″

ARMS ½″ DIA. SCREWED INTO HUB & LOCK-NUTTED

HUB DISC TO REPLACE OR BOLT TO FLYWHEEL

BOLTS FITTED WITH SPRING WASHERS & LOCKNUTS

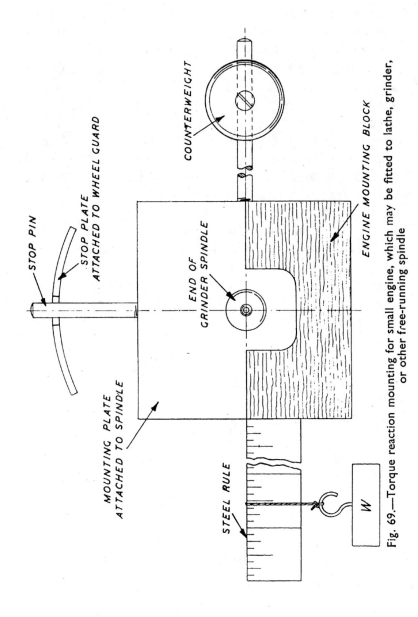

STOP PIN

STOP PLATE
ATTACHED TO WHEEL GUARD

COUNTERWEIGHT

ENGINE MOUNTING BLOCK

END OF
GRINDER SPINDLE

MOUNTING PLATE
ATTACHED TO SPINDLE

STEEL RULE

W

Fig. 69.—Torque reaction mounting for small engine, which may be fitted to lathe, grinder, or other free-running spindle

but if there is the least doubt about the cleanliness of the oil used to fill the tank or sump, it should be filtered or syphoned into a perfectly clean can or bottle, the latter for preference, as it enables one to see the condition of the oil which it contains.

Where water cooling is employed, tanks or radiators should be filled with clean and preferably soft water. Pond water used for cooling boat engines is not distinguished for its purity, and gratings are necessary to prevent foreign matter from fouling the jackets, but, even with the greatest care, it is often impossible to prevent mud or sand entering and depositing in awkward places. The best way to avoid trouble from this cause is to flush out the jackets with a hose from the water main at frequent intervals or whenever there is reason to believe the passages may be partially blocked. Sometimes hot water or the use of chemical solvents may be desirable to remove hard deposits.

Air filters are not at all common fittings on model engines, and in many cases the slight restriction of air flow which they inevitably cause would be undesirable in an engine which needs to develop its utmost power. The best way to ensure clean air is to arrange that the air inlet, or an extension trunk fitted to it, is situated so as to take air which is not likely to pick up unwanted matter, either foreign or liquid. In this respect, it may be noted that boat engines are often stopped, and not infrequently seriously damaged, by spray or "green water" which gets into the air intake. This can be almost entirely prevented by a judicious choice of the intake position, preferably below the scuttle or deck coaming, and this precaution will often save the engine, even when the boat capsizes and sinks.

Diagnosing Faults

Even the best engines occasionally go wrong, and one of the objects of learning all one can about them is to be able to forestall and prevent most of these troubles and, on the infrequent occasions when they inevitably occur, to detect and correct them. Anyone who has had experience with full-sized engines will learn to recognise most of the prevailing ailments of small models, as the symptoms are generally similar, but they are often more difficult to distinguish, and sometimes baffle even the most experienced investigators.

It is fairly safe to say that the majority of running troubles and failures in all kinds of petrol engines are due to faults in either the fuel supply or the ignition. Some of the symptoms of disorder in these functions are similar, and may easily be confused. Either of them can cause failure of the engine to start or to keep running ; poor acceleration, loss of power or speed, misfiring or rough running. There are, however, generally some clues which help to enable one to distinguish which of the two functions is giving trouble.

Partial or complete failure of the fuel supply generally has less sudden or violent effects than ignition trouble ; in other words, it is indicated by " petering out," " hunting," more or less rhythmic misfiring, or general lassitude. Ignition trouble, on the other hand, generally cuts out the engine abruptly, perhaps in alternate bursts, as if the engine were switched on and off, but more often by fits and starts, with no rhythmic pattern.

Fuel supply should always be checked by making sure that there is no interruption of the flow to the jet, and that the latter is not obstructed by foreign matter. Variable jets can often be cleared by opening the jet more widely for a moment. With some fuels it is possible for an incrustation to form inside the jet, which gradually reduces the effective aperture. Engines lubricated by petroil, if left standing for some time, often refuse to start because the jet is obstructed by congealed oil. The use of an oil which is not soluble in the fuel may result in the formation of globules which prevent the fuel passing the jet as effectively as a ball valve, and the same effect is produced by water in the fuel. Where rubber pipes or connections are used in the fuel feed line, minute particles of the rubber are often dissolved away and carried into the jet to form a perpetual source of trouble.

Ignition trouble has its most common source in weak or run-down batteries, which should always be checked up before starting a run ; but the use of a voltmeter is not always a sound guide to their condition, as the voltage of a battery may be superficially correct on open circuit, but may drop almost to zero when it is called upon to deliver a heavy current. A check of the spark at the plug lead will determine at once whether the ignition system is in working order. The sparking plug is another common offender, and the fact that it shows a spark at the points when tested outside the cylinder does not always prove that it sparks under compression. One or two spare plugs, known to be in good working order, should always be kept handy if possible. Dirty or pitted contact-breaker points, a weak breaker spring, or imperfect connections anywhere in the circuit are often responsible for bad misfiring or failure of the engine to start ; a less common fault, but one which should not be left out of consideration, is wear or maladjustment of the contacts, which prevents them from closing, or, on the other hand, wear of the cam or fibre pad so that they do not open. A faulty condenser will result in a very weak spark or none at all ; it is sometimes indicated by excessive sparking at the contact points.

Poor compression is a frequent cause of unsatisfactory running or loss of power in small engines, and it may not uncommonly make starting difficult or impossible. The most obvious cause of this fault is an inaccurate cylinder, or bad fitting of the piston, or its rings, but it may also be due to leaky valves or leaking joints at the cylinder head, valve caps or sparking plug.

Excessive friction is sometimes set up by distortion of the piston or cylinder, overstrain of working parts, or faulty lubrication, and this will result in laboured running or refusal to take load. Derangement of ignition or valve timing often produces trouble which is difficult to diagnose, but a quick rough check-up is generally possible without dismantling the engine. The effects of overheating or mechanical breakdown are generally too obvious to escape notice.

The most baffling trouble—and not by any means an infrequent one—is that of the engine which refuses to work, although everything appears to be in perfect order. When this occurs in a new engines, the design is frequently blamed, but more often it is due to combination of very small defects in detail or adjustment. In such cases one can only proceed by a process of elimination, and a great deal of patience is called for. The temperamental individual who is liable to throw tools in all directions and stamp on the engine is hardly likely to be very successful in dealing with this trouble !

Adjustments

In large engines it is common practice to leave the user as few running adjustments as possible, but this policy is hardly practicable in model engines, and success in their use depends very largely in understanding the effect of various adjustments and handling them delicately. The most important adjustment on most small engines is the variable jet screw, which often has to be used as a running control, and in any case has the most far-reaching effect on engine performance. One advantage of using an automatic carburettor is that it enables the best jet settings to be found and permanently maintained, though this is often neglected by users, who fail to realise the advantages of these carburettors, as a result. Slight readjustments of the jets and other adjustments of these carburettors are, however, necessary to compensate for changes in climatic conditions or to suit different fuels.

In the case of two-stroke engines fitted with simple carburettors, it is usual to start with the mixture on the rich side and, as the engine warms up, to reduce the jet aperture until the engine two-strokes properly. Alternatively, when a fixed or pre-set jet is employed, a control may be fitted to the air intake, so that a rich mixture for starting may be obtained by partially strangling the air supply. This is rather the better method, but often it is desirable to adjust both the jet and the air control, especially if it is desired to regulate the engine speed and still keep the mixture at the correct strength. A four-stroke engine will fire evenly over a much wider range of mixture strength than a two-stroke, and it may not be so easy to tell when the correct mixture has been found, simply by listening to the beat of the engine. But with any type of engine, over-richness of the mixture is indicated by a general fluffiness of running, a tendency to surge or " hunt," and black smoke at the exhaust. This must not be confused with the blue smoke caused by partial combustion of lubricating oil. A considerable excess of fuel will very effectively prevent an engine from starting, and failure to realise how fine an adjustment of the fuel supply is required is one of the most prolific causes of the beginner's difficulties with small engines. A two-stroke engine which has been over-fed with fuel will often collect a quantity of it in the crankcase, which must then be completely emptied and " aired out " by turning the engine for some time with fuel shut off before normal conditions can be restored. Explosions at the exhaust port or in the silencer are symptoms of over-rich mixture.

Too weak a mixture, on the other hand, tends to fierce running, racing on light load, " spitting back " in the air intake, and overheating. The combustion rate is delayed by either rich or weak mixture, and as a result it will continue after the exhaust port or valve is open, so that a flame is visible unless a long exhaust pipe is fitted. But in the case of a rich mixture the flame will be long, yellow and smoky, whereas weak mixture causes a short blue flame. The coughing or spitting back caused by weak mixture is an entirely different symptom to a backfire caused by incorrect ignition timing, or an open-port explosion due to a sticky exhaust or inlet valve.

Ignition timing is also generally adjusted by observing its effect on the running of the engine, and it is fairly easy to tell

N

when it is most suitable for the particular conditions of load and speed which exist at the time. Most engines have a fair latitude of tolerance in this respect, and will run over a fair range of load and speed without altering the ignition timing adjustment. Some engines have been run successfully with no provision whatever for advancing or retarding the ignition. On the other hand, there are few intelligent users of model petrol engines who would willingly dispense with the ignition control, and with many engines, especially two-strokes, it is possible to use it as a speed control over a fair range.

Small engines rarely need to have the ignition retarded later than top dead centre and will often take advance up to as much as 45 degrees earlier than this point, at full speed. Late ignition causes laboured, heavy running of the engine and prevents full speed being obtained, while too much advance makes it reluctant to take full load and may delay recovery if speed is temporarily lost by heavy overloading, or even cause the engine to stall or " conk out." The maximum rate of acceleration under load is usually obtained by retarding the ignition slightly, and re-advancing it gradually as the engine picks up. Backfiring is not very liable to occur in small engines unless far too much advance is used when starting up. In some types of two-stroke engines, designed to run in either direction, it is possible to reverse the engine by a deliberate backfire. While the engine is running on normal advance, the ignition is switched off until the speed drops considerably. Just short of stalling point, contact is again closed by the switch, and, if conditions have been correctly judged, the resultant backfire will reverse the engine, which will continue to run in the other direction if the contact breaker is suitably designed.

Improving Engine Performance

As every enthusiastic motor-cyclist knows, one of the most fascinating features of the petrol engine is the scope which it offers for improvement of performance by careful attention to

details. This characteristic is, if anything, even more pronounced in model engines, few of which, as originally constructed, reach the limit of their performance right away,
however well designed and made. In fact, it is usual for
engines to improve automatically for some time after their
initial run, due to the gradual reduction of friction as the
working parts get run in, and this process takes much longer
than is commonly believed. Even when the parts are finished
to the highest degree of accuracy and polish which can possibly
be obtained, a certain amount of running in is always necessary,
and, during this period, great care should be taken to ensure
adequate lubrication, and to avoid overworking the engine in
any way. The future success of the engine may be very considerably influenced by the way it is handled during the early
stages.

After running-in is complete, the engine should settle down
to a steady power output until its performance is impaired
by wear of the working parts, but this should take quite a
long time if it is well made of the correct materials. Some
engines produce their best performance at a stage in their
career when they might logically be expected to deserve
" pensioning off."

No attempt should be made to modify the construction of
an engine, with a view to improving its performance, until it
has been carefully and thoroughly run in, and all its controls
and adjustments have been fully mastered. If an engine can
be given a constant load, such as with an airscrew or fan brake,
its speed at this load should be carefully checked over a number of runs and used to gauge the effect of any alterations
made to it. An increase in the effciency of the engine, however
produced, must obviously result in an increase of speed for a
given load, or, on the other hand, will enable the same speed
to be maintained with an increased load.

Alteration of valve or port timing is often resorted to as a
means of improving performance, but needs a good deal of
patience and perseverance to ensure obtaining the best

possible results. In a four-stroke engine, this can be done by changing the cams—merely altering their position is not usually very profitable unless they were originally timed incorrectly, as any advantage gained by earlier opening of the valve may be cancelled by earlier closing, while the same applies if the valve timing is retarded. There is unlimited scope for experiment in cam design, not only in respect of finding the best possible timing and period of opening, but also the best form of cam to make the most of the opening period, and to lift and close the valve with the minimum mechanical effort. There is reason to believe that the purely mechanical aspect of cam design may be far more important than lift, or angle of opening, in influencing engine performance.

The timing of two-stroke engines can only be altered by opening out the ports, and thus any alteration made is practically immutable, except by changing major working parts. With a four-stroke engine, it is always possible to revert to the *status quo* by replacing the original cams, or re-setting them to the initial timing, but, once the ports of a two-stroke have been altered, the original timing can only be restored by fitting a new cylinder or by making involved alterations to other parts. For this reason, any port alterations on a two-stroke should be tackled cautiously, and only a very little at a time, the effect of each stage being carefully checked by running tests.

Improvement in high-speed performance can nearly always be effected by reducing the weight of reciprocating parts, if this can be done without dangerously reducing their strength. Pistons can often be pared away internally by milling or rotary-filing until they consist of nothing more than a thin shell, but it should be remembered that this reduces their rate of heat conductivity, and thus may limit the engine power which can be sustained without overheating.

It is often possible to reduce the weight of a connecting rod quite safely, such as by making it hollow, in the case of a circular-section rod, or milling grooves in the sides of a flat rod, if such operations have not already been done. The substitution of a light alloy rod for a steel or bronze rod will often enable a substantial reduction of weight to be made. Solid gudgeon pins are unnecessarily heavy, a large-diameter hollow pin being always better than a smaller solid one.

Altering the weight of working parts will affect the balance of the engine, which will afterwards require readjustment. Other methods of improving engine performance will be described under the heading of " Tuning."

Balancing

The usual form of single-cylinder engine cannot be perfectly balanced. A reciprocating mass moving in a certain direction can only be balanced by an equal mass moving in the opposite direction, in the same plane, at the same speed. This condition can only be attained in opposed-piston engines, which are necessarily more complicated in construction than the usual type of engine. The latter, therefore, can only be partially balanced by attaching counterweights to the crankshaft opposite the crankpin, but these have a rotary motion and move at a constant velocity, while the reciprocating parts have a variable speed from zero at the dead centres to maximum at the middle of the stroke. As a result, correct balance could only be obtained at one instant of the stroke by this method, and in practice balancing consists of a somewhat haphazard compromise, and is mainly a matter of arriving at the magnitude and direction of unbalanced forces which can best be tolerated by the engine. If no balance weights at all are fitted, a vibration is set up in the same plane as (but opposite to) the piston stroke ; balance weights sufficiently massive to cancel this completely, on the other hand, result in a vibration at right angles to this plane, i.e. in the plane of the crank motion at the dead centres. Something between the two extremes gives the best results, varying to a certain extent with the construction and method of mounting of the engine and the speed at which it runs. The usual practice is to balance out about half the reciprocating weight, plus all unbalanced rotating weight, which includes the crankpin and lower half of the connecting rod.

To balance a small engine, the procedure is as follows : First weigh the piston carefully, including the rings and gudgeon pin. Next weigh the two ends of the connecting rod separately, keeping it suspended horizontally while doing so. The weight of the piston and the small end of the rod is then divided by two and added to the full weight of the other end

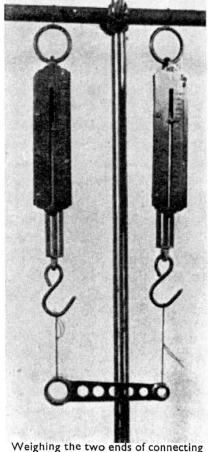

Weighing the two ends of connecting rod

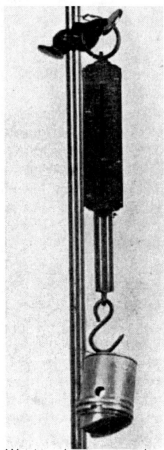

Weighing the piston, complete with rings and gudgeon pin

of the rod. Weights equal to this amount should be made up in any convenient way, such as in the form of shot or sand, which can be applied in a scale pan or hung on a weight hanger. The crankshaft is now mounted on horizontal knife-edges, carefully levelled both ways so that it can roll freely. Steel rules or the backs of hacksaw blades, clamped to suitable mounting blocks, will serve for knife-edges. The flywheel may be fitted to the shaft provided that it is known to be in balance itself, as it has a steadying effect on the shaft. The weights determined as above are now hung from the crankpin, and the weight of the balance weights should be adjusted by cutting away or adding to them until the pin will remain poised in mid-position, with no inclination for the shaft to roll either way.

Even when balanced carefully in this way, there is no positive guarantee that some readjustment may not be

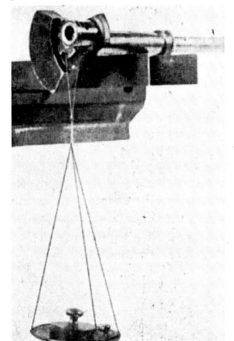

necessary to cope with particular running conditions, and the best results are generally only obtained after some experiment.

The balance weight or weights should always be very securely attached to the crankshaft, if not actually integral with it, and should be as close to the plane of the piston as possible. On no account should an attempt be

Adjusting the balance weight on crankshaft to correspond with calculated weight

made to balance an engine by counterweighting the flywheel or other rotating parts outside the bearings. Placing the balance weight at a distance along the shaft from the plane of the piston will result in an unbalanced " couple " which may be more troublesome than the effect it is intended to counteract. This is the reason why side-by-side twin engines, with the cranks at 180 degrees, are often more difficult to balance than single-cylinder engines, though one might imagine that one piston would automatically balance the other. They do not do so, however, simply because their planes of motion are some distance removed from each other, so that the unbalanced forces see-saw about the centre of the engine, which tends to rock longitudinally as a result.

It will be fairly clear that the subject of balancing is a very complicated one, and only the bare outline of it can be given here, but it is hoped that the constructor will find the information helpful in understanding at least the nature of the problems involved.

Compression Ratio

Most model petrol engines give their best results, except when specially tuned for racing and running on special fuels, with a moderate compression ratio, according to the running speed for which they are designed. Low-speed stationary engines may be run most efficiently on a compression ratio as low as 4 to 1, and moderate-duty engines for aircraft, proto-type boats and the like rarely call for a higher ratio than 6 to 1. It is possible to use much higher ratios than this with ordinary fuels, but by no means so easy to obtain real benefit from them. Even in racing engines the advantages of high compression can only be realised if all other factors in the functioning of the engine are working efficiently, and in harmony with each other.

Increasing the compression ratio has the effect of causing a proportionate rise in the combustion temperature and pressure when the mixture is ignited, and also speeds up the rate of combustion. Theoretically, at least, this should result in an increase of power, and a better performance at high speed. Unfortunately, however, the result of increasing the working pressure increases the power absorbed by the engine in pumping and compressing the mixture, and the proportion of loss caused by any leakage past the piston and valves ; the bearing thrusts are also greater, causing an increase of mechanical friction. The higher temperature does not necessarily make the engine run hotter ; in fact, the *waste* heat should be reduced, but the sparking plug is more likely to become overheated, and the rejection of the gases at higher pressure and temperature is liable to burn the exhaust valve.

It sometimes happens, therefore, that, when an attempt is made to improve engine performance by raising the compression ratio, the practical gain may be less than might be expected. Sometimes an originally docile engine becomes fierce and temperamental ; a simple method of lubrication may be found inadequate to cope with increased bearing loads ; and acceleration from low speed under load may be adversely affected. One should always take into account these possible disadvantages and not jump to the conclusion that high compression is an infallible means of increasing engine power ; but, when discreetly exploited, in an engine of suitable design and sound construction, it is an important factor, in conjunction with other methods, in attaining this end.

Special Fuels

Model petrol engines are often believed to have a fastidious taste in fuels, but this is not strictly true. In some cases specially volatile fuels are employed to facilitate starting of these engines from cold, but such measures are not normally necessary, and they will run quite well on ordinary grades of motor spirit, or even very low-grade fuels in many cases.

Most small engines are practically immune from the troubles which arise in large engines due to the use of unsuitable fuels, as the small volume of the combustion chamber gives little opportunity for the violent effects of detonation to make themselves felt. Combustion knock, or " pinking," is very rarely encountered. Nevertheless, it would be a mistake to assume that differences in fuels have no effect on the performance of model engines. In nearly all cases they will show some particular preference in this respect, not always for any apparent logical reason.

It is sometimes stated that high-compression engines demand special fuels ; but in model engines it might be more correct to say that some fuels can only be used to good effect in engines of high compression. This applies to racing fuels of high octane value and, in particular, those containing benzole or alcohol.

One advantage of alcohol as a fuel for high performance engines is that it requires less oxygen for complete combustion than " straight " petrol ; consequently, it is possible to consume a larger quantity of it to useful effect in the amount of air which can be drawn into a cylinder of a given capacity. Some alcohols contain a certain percentage of water, the vapour of which can be exploited to damp violent combustion and to act as an internal coolant. Special fuels sometimes allow a wider range of mixture strength to be tolerated, but, generally speaking, high performance can only be obtained by the most meticulous carburation adjustment. In this respect, again, the model petrol engine user must not jump to conclusions as to the benefits which can be obtained, and to regard any particular " fancy " fuel as an " elixir of life " to the racing engine is a dangerous fallacy.

It is impossible to lay down any definite rules as to what compression ratio should be used with a given fuel, as the characteristics of engines vary enormously, but it may be stated that racing model engines have been run successfully on " straight " or standard commercial fuels at $8\frac{1}{2}$ to 1 compression ratio, " blended " fuels (mostly petrol-benzole mixtures) at 10 to 1, and special alcohol or other racing fuels at 15 to 1. There is no claim that these figures represent the best possible compression ratios in either case.

Tuning for High Efficiency

In the literal sense, the process of "tuning" an engine for racing implies fine adjustment and harmonious co-ordination of all its functions. Another very important consideration in this process is the reduction of friction to the minimum, whether it be in the mechanical working parts, in the flow of gases through the passages, or drag caused by the clinging of viscous oil to internal parts in rapid motion. Tuning can never under any circumstances be done in a hurry ; a great deal of patience is necessary to find and eliminate the limiting factors in the performance of the engine and to check up on the results of modifications and readjustments.

Mechanical friction should be the first thing to be dealt with. In addition to the most careful running-in of a new engine, constant observation of the state of its working parts will show up anything which interferes with smooth and effortless running, such as high spots caused by minor distortion of the piston or cylinder, which should be lapped down or eased with a very fine file. Progressive distortion which refuses to be disposed of by a few applications of this treatment generally indicates that there is some error in the design of the part concerned, and the appropriate action should be taken. If shafts or bearings show a persistent tendency to score or "pick up," this may be due to a wrong choice of bearing materials or shafts too soft for the load they have to carry ; on the other hand, it may indicate inadequate lubrication or unsuitable oil. Surfaces too hard to be scraped or filed may be smoothed with a fine India or Turkey oilstone slip. A fine carborundum slip may be used for more drastic treatment ; the use of emery cloth or loose abrasives is not generally advised in a finished engine, and in any case great care should be exercised to remove the least trace of abrasive or metal dust from the parts which have been dealt with before reassembly.

Ball or roller races cannot, in themselves, be improved by any after-treatment, and no attempt should be made to interfere with them in any way ; but in many cases the original fitting of them to shafts and housings can be improved. Too tight fitting, either inside or outside, will tend to make the race bind, but in petrol engines it is generally advisable to fit the race slightly tighter than usual, as the races work at a fairly high temperature and thus loosen slightly under working conditions. When two ball races are fitted to a shaft, only one should have fixed end location, the other being free to move endwise to allow for expansion of the shaft. Loose races can only be dealt with by bushing the housings or building up the shafts by electro-deposition. Sometimes a race may be slightly out of square, through careless fitting or distortion, and this is fatal to efficient running. Bearings of any kind should work quite freely and smoothly with no suspicion of " lumpiness " anywhere.

Minor engine bearings, such as camshafts, valve rockers, etc., should all receive due attention, and gearwheels adjusted to mesh freely and run as silently as possible—noise in gears is a sure sign of inefficiency. Cam surfaces should be smooth and bright, and any spots which show evidence of excessive loading may be eased with an oilstone ; rubbing surfaces of cams and tappets should all be glass-hard.

Having exhausted all possibilities in eliminating mechanical friction, the gas passages should now be dealt with. Any roughness in their internal surfaces should be scrupulously removed and sharp corners faired off. Abrupt changes of shape or diameter of passages should be avoided. Some engine tuners will take great pains to polish a valve port, but fail to notice that when the pipe with which it communicates is bolted up, the two bores are considerably out of line. Internal parts exposed to flame should have no sharp corners anywhere, and high polish of these parts helps to prevent the adhesion of carbon deposits.

The inside of the crankcase should be as smooth as possible

to prevent both air and oil friction. Everyone knows that the crankcase of a two-stroke acts as an air pump, but it is less universally realised that similar air displacement takes place in a four-stroke, and also that there is generally more oil present in the latter, which is capable of acting as a hydraulic brake. High polish and rounding-off of corners helps to reduce friction in either type of engine. Never forget that friction is the arch-enemy to efficiency in all petrol engines, and the smaller they are, the more important it becomes to eliminate it wherever possible ; it is futile to attempt to tune an engine which wastes its power in laboriously turning its own internal parts.

All working adjustments of the engine call for more and more meticulous adjustment as its speed and performance improve and, unless one is prepared to take the necessary trouble to set them really accurately, it is definitely better to put up with a " woolly " engine in which adjustments are less critical. Many users who attempt to tune engines seem to lack the skill or the patience to carry out the involved operation of setting the various adjustments in complete co-ordination to produce the best engine performance.

If it is not practicable to preserve the set position of the important adjustments, their positions should be carefully marked, so that they can be reverted to without " searching." It is a sound policy to have as few adjustments as possible which have to be manipulated for starting and controlling the speed of any engine, although some of the most skilful exponents of racing have employed engines having a formidable array of running controls. In the excitement and stress of a keenly contested race, however, one is very liable to " muff " or forget essential adjustments, and most operators will find that the fewer they are the better.

Increase of compression and the use of special fuels will generally necessitate re-setting of adjustments, and still more care in their manipulation. Success in racing with model petrol engines is often attributed to good luck, but, though this may be true in a few isolated cases, it is far more often the reward of patience, perseverance and the genius which is aptly described as " an infinite capacity for taking pains."

" Dont's " for Engine Tuners

Don't imagine you can find a short cut to engine tuning. It is doubtful whether any engine was ever properly tuned in a hurry, and the stories sometimes related of engines being completed only the day before the race, and beating all comers on their first run, should be taken with a grain of salt.

Don't try to remove friction by making everything a sloppy fit. This may have the very opposite effect by making it impossible to maintain oil films between heavily-loaded surfaces. Large clearances are frequently necessary to compensate for expansion or unavoidable deflection ; but they should be regarded as a necessary evil rather than a virtue.

Don't jump to conclusions about causes and effects, but check everything by careful and patient observation. Even an expert may fail to identify faults correctly, or to locate the " bottleneck " in the engine performance, when making a rapid diagnosis.

Don't think that big ports, high compression, hard plugs, and " fancy " fuels constitute a universal and infallible recipe for maximum performance. In many cases they only complicate the issues, and should never be indulged in until everything else possible has been done to improve power output.

Don't make the common mistake of thinking that a terrifying exhaust crackle is a proof of super-performance. Noise is always a sign of waste in some form or other, and the inevitable noise associated with a racing engine must be put on the debit side, not the credit. While a powerful engine must of necessity be rather noisy, it does not follow that every noisy engine is powerful.

Don't confuse the ability to " rev " at incredible speed with real efficiency. Every engine develops its maximum power at a speed well below its maximum r.p.m., and one of the primary objects of tuning is to make the power curve rise with the speed as far as possible. Although the majority of inefficient engines are sluggish and fail to attain high speed under any circumstances, mere high speed at little or no load does not prove high engine performance.

Mr. J. Cruickshank testing a 6 c.c. "Atom Minor" engine on the torque reaction dynamometer illustrated in Fig. 69

CHAPTER XII

POSSIBLE FUTURE DEVELOPMENTS

MODEL engineers are for ever seeking new worlds to conquer, and, despite the fact that there is no lack of unsolved problems in the simplest and most conventional types of engines, many designers and constructors attempt to keep up to date with, or even to anticipate, the latest developments in full-size practice. There is no doubt that the advancement of design offers a very fruitful and extremely interesting field for the enterprise of the model engineer, but it calls for the utmost patience, determination and intelligence. Every new departure of design introduces new, and sometimes unexpected, problems ; in many cases it takes many years of patient development to realise the potential advantages of what appears, at first sight, to be an obvious and unquestionable advantage.

By way of example, take the case of the sleeve-valve engine, which was invented very early in the history of the internal combustion engine ; of the two best-known examples, the Knight double-sleeve and the Burt-McCollum single-sleeve, the former was exploited for several years by the Daimler Company and others, but eventually discarded because of practical difficulties. The latter was also taken up by several firms, including the Argyll Car Company, Messrs. Barr & Stroud, Ltd., and others, but it is only in recent years that its practical merit has been proved in the large Bristol and Napier aircraft engines. Another idea which is just as old in conception, the rotary-valve engine, is still in its teething stage even now. These examples are given not to deter the intending experimenter, but to point out that there is no short cut to advanced design, and improvement in performance is more often obtainable by close detail study and perseverance with well-tried principles of design than by exploring totally new fields.

In this chapter it is proposed to review the most promising lines of development which are likely to be explored in the immediate future, indicating as far as possible their particular advantages, problems and difficulties, also the fallacies which are often entertained regarding them.

Improved Two-Stroke Engines

In considering the possibility of developing and improving this popular type of engine, it should be remembered that the features which have contributed perhaps more than anything else to its practical success are its simplicity and high mechanical efficiency, and most attempts to improve it, except in small details, are liable to complicate it, or to result in increased working friction. Many devices which have been considered obvious improvements have proved to be partial or complete failures in practice for this reason. In the development of full-sized two-strokes, cheap production is always a powerful incentive to simplicity, but even when there is no restriction in cost, real improvement has more often been found in the direction of metallurgy and workmanship than in functional principles.

The "flat-top" engine, which does not complicate construction and has at least potential mechanical and thermal advantages, is likely to become more popular among amateur constructors, though its development calls for patient experiment, and its ultimate advantages may not amount to so much as they do in larger engines.

Mechanically-operated valve gear of any kind has not, so far, been found very helpful in two-stroke engines, but there is some possibility that it might be developed, in connection with supercharging, to increase power output. The rotary admission valve, however, which does not increase complica-

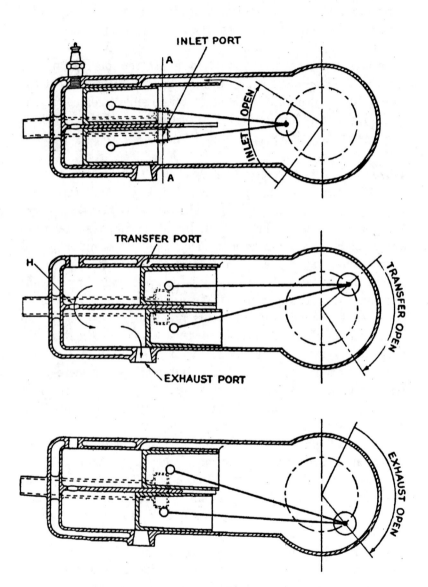

Fig. 70.—Diagram illustrating the principle of the "split single" or "double-barrelled" two-stroke engine

tion or friction to any marked extent, is nearly always an asset and can be recommended on any small engine. Improvements in the scavenging of the two-stroke engine are always desirable, but, apart from detail work on the ports, passages and piston design, practically the only way in which this can be done is to introduce end-to-end scavenging by the use of two pistons uncovering ports at either end of the cylinder. The "straight" double-piston engine, however, introduces awkward constructional problems, and the more common development of this idea is to bend the cylinder into an inverted U so that the pistons work side by side in parallel planes. Sometimes the connecting rods from the two pistons

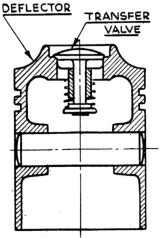

DEFLECTOR TRANSFER VALVE

Fig. 71.—An automatic transfer valve fitted to a two-stroke engine piston

are jointed to work on the same crankpin, or they may work on separate throws of the same crankshaft. In other cases two crankshafts, geared together to run in opposite directions, are employed. One feature of this type of engine is that the pistons may be set slightly out of phase (in the case of forked or articulated connecting rods this takes place automatically), and thus the exhaust ports, controlled by one piston, may have

a lead both in opening and closing over the transfer ports
controlled by the other piston. This results in more efficient
charging, with less wastage of the charge, and also enables
the engine to be supercharged if desired.

Automatic valves have sometimes been used in two-stroke
engines, particularly for the admission of the charge to the
crankcase, but also occasionally for transferring it into the
cylinder. In some engines, the transfer valve has been located
in the head of the piston, but this has often resulted in
mechanical trouble or burning of the valve. The idea has,
however, been revived in recent years by using the form of
piston shown in Fig. 72, in which the outer shell of the piston
is capable of movement relative to the inner portion, which
carries the gudgeon pin bosses and also a conical valve, which
is kept closed by pressure in the cylinder during the com-

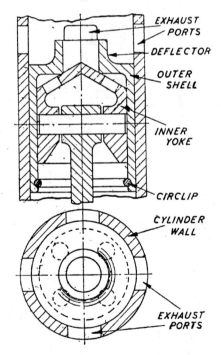

Fig. 72.—A novel form of piston-head transfer valve

pression and firing strokes of the engine. As soon as the exhaust ports are uncovered by the top edge of the piston, however, the pressure on the latter is relaxed and its motion stops, allowing the inner portion to finish its travel alone and thus open the valve. Some form of limiting device is fitted inside the piston to prevent the two parts becoming entirely separated when the engine is not working normally.

Four-Stroke Engines

In full-size practice, the four-stroke engine is most popular for high performance work, and in consequence, more attention is paid to the advancement of its design ; but it does not always follow that the most modern features of full-sized engines are applicable with equal advantage to model engines. Many of the developments in design in recent years have been in connection with valve gearing, with a view to obtaining better " breathing " or volumetric efficiency of the engine at high speed. While this is also very desirable in a model engine, it is of no real advantage if it increases the power necessary to drive the valve gear, which is always greater in proportion to total power as the size of the engine is reduced. Such features as radial valves, multiple valves, and overhead camshafts are often tried out in model engines, and may be reasonably successful if detail design and execution are good; but there is little real evidence that they are much better than the simplest forms of valve gear.

Increasing the number of cylinders is always a dubious feature in small engines designed for high efficiency, the main reason again being that mechanical efficiency is reduced, but another potential source of trouble or loss of power is imperfect mixture distribution. Some difficulty may also be experienced in obtaining efficient ignition at high speed, because of the multiplication of the number of sparks required in a given time. This does not, however, imply that thoroughly satisfactory performance, for anything other than the most arduous racing conditions, is not possible from multi-cylinder engines ; they are, moreover, an extremely attractive proposition to the constructor who admires prototype design and fine workmanship. For sheer power, however, it is very difficult to improve on the single-cylinder engine in any size likely to be considered within the scope of this book.

The following features of design, which are applicable to both four-stroke and two-stroke engines, will now be reviewed in relation to their promise of actual increase of performance or other practical advantages in small engines.

Sleeve Valves

The particular advantage of any form of ported valve (whether it has a reciprocating, rotating or combined motion) over the more usual poppet valve, is that it is capable of controlling the valve events positively at any rate of speed, and can be kept reasonably cool, or at least at an even temperature, so that distortion or other thermal trouble can be avoided. In the case of the sleeve valve, however, some difficulty has often been experienced in obtaining the necessary accuracy of the internal and external surfaces and maintaining it during the working life of the engine. Friction is liable to be fairly heavy, particularly if lubrication conditions are not perfect, and the mechanical means of operating the sleeve are liable to introduce complication in design and difficulty in balancing.

It will be observed that these characteristics are such 'that, in a small engine, the disadvantages of the sleeve valve rather tend to outweigh the advantages. The writer has always been of the opinion that the sleeve valve works under the most favourable conditions in a large engine, and this appears to be borne out by the modern development of this type of valve. Nevertheless, it is quite possible to make a small sleeve valve engine which will at least reproduce the smooth running and mechanical quietness of large engines of this type. Successful engines of this type have been built by Mr. C. Brinton and Mr. G. Noble.

A 30 c.c. " Cross " type rotary-valve engine
built by Mr. B. Kerswell

Rotary Valves

Apart from the use of rotary valves for admission on two-stroke engines, where both the temperature and pressure are very moderate and mechanical arrangements are of the simplest, the rotary type of valve presents problems and potential advantages somewhat similar to those of the sleeve valve. The surface area of most rotary valves is, however, comparatively small, so that friction can be reduced and, as they generally have a continuous rotary motion, their operation is simpler and less power is lost in inertia than in the case of the sleeve valve. Problems of keeping the valve gastight and properly lubricated under working conditions are, however, greater and constitute the greatest practical objection to this type of valve at present.

Two types of rotary valve in course of development in full-size practice which have attracted the attention of several model engineers are the Cross cylindrical valve and the Aspin conical valve. The former works externally to the cylinder head in a housing at right angles to the cylinder bore, communicating with the latter through a port ; inlet and exhaust passages are connected to the two ends of the valve casing. The Aspin valve, on the other hand, works inside the cylinder head and embodies a cavity which forms the actual combustion space ; a single port leading from this cavity communicates with exhaust and inlet ports in the head, angularly located so as to ensure correct timing.

Both types of valves embody many ingenious features of design, including pressure-balancing and lubricating devices, and have been shown in practice to be capable of extremely high efficiency. Their principles appear to be applicable with more or less equal advantage to models and, if the practical problems above mentioned can be successfully solved, they offer a promising line of development for small high-performance engines.

A 30-c.c. Cross-type rotary-valve engine was made some years ago by Mr. Kerswell, but no details of its performance

A 2½ c.c. Aspin-type rotary-valve engine constructed by Mr. N. Boero

are available. The Aspin type of valve has been exploited by several model engineers, one of its most successful exponents being Mr. N. Boero, who has produced a $2\frac{1}{2}$-c.c. engine and a 30-c.c. engine, both having this feature.

Supercharging

The " breathing " efficiency of an engine which falls off badly at high speed can be boosted by feeding the mixture to the inlet valve under pressure, and this very obvious means of increasing engine performance has attracted a good deal of attention in recent years.* Unfortunately, however, it is not so easy to carry out as it may seem, and many practical problems have arisen in applying supercharging with advantage to small engines. As usual, the greatest difficulties are in respect of mechanical efficiency. Any form of pump used in forcibly feeding the mixture to the engine must necessarily take a certain amount of power to drive it, and in assessing the net gain in power thus produced, this power must be deducted from the extra internal engine power obtained by the supercharge. If the net gain is small, it may not justify the extra complication of fitting supercharging gear, to say nothing of the extra wear and tear on all working parts of the engine. Carburation problems are liable to be accentuated, and special pressure-balancing devices for the feed and air intake pipes are often found necessary ; ignition conditions also become more exacting, calling for " harder " plugs and higher-voltage ignition equipment.

In some experiments conducted by Mr. D. H. Chaddock some years ago, in collaboration with the writer, careful measurements of the engine power output and the power

---

* Generally speaking, the term " supercharging " applies to any means of supplementing the ability of the engine to induce its own charge by aspiration ; but a distinction must be made between methods which simply compensate for deficiencies in volumetric efficiency, and " pressure boost " systems, in which the supercharger supplies a greater volume of mixture than the cylinder capacity, so that the pressure in the induction system is well above that of the atmosphere.

required to drive the supercharger resulted in the conclusion that it is extremely difficult to obtain a high enough mechanical efficiency in the latter to enable it to be used to any real advantage at all. While this does not necessarily condemn the supercharger finally, it indicates that the problems involved in its application are by no means as simple as some designers seem to think, and that they cannot be disposed of without a good deal of practical research.

Supercharging can be effected in various ways, such as by means of " displacement " or reciprocating blowers, by engine-driven rotary blowers, and by external blowers operated by exhaust gases or waste heat. The displacement blower, entailing the need for a piston and cylinder, appears on the face of it to be the most inefficient of all, but if the blower piston can be combined with, or made an extension to, the main piston, it may possibly serve as a crosshead to reduce side-thrust on the latter and thus become a mechanical asset. This principle has been somewhat ex-

A Zoller type supercharger for 30 c.c. engines built by Mr. D. H. Chaddock

tensively applied to two-stroke engines, in the form of the
" stepped " piston, which may be used as an alternative
or a supplement to crankcase compression ; but it is advisable
to point out that the orthodox form of port-controlled
two-stroke cannot be truly supercharged, though its breathing
at high speed may be improved in this way.

The simplest form of displacement supercharger applicable
to four-stroke engines of two (or more) cylinders consists of
using a closed crankcase and using it as a pump in much the
same way as in two-stroke engines. In the case of an engine
such as a horizontally-opposed twin, in which the pistons
move in opposite directions and the cylinders fire on alternate
revolutions, the two pistons contribute to crankcase displacement, which is used to charge one cylinder on each revolution.
If volumetric efficiency of the pump were 100 per cent., each
cylinder would thus receive double its normal charge, but in
actual fact nothing like this amount of supercharge has ever
been realised in practice. The elimination of a separate
cylinder does not by any means cancel out mechanical loss,
and the use of a closed crankcase imposes definite limitations
in respect of lubrication. In practice, this method of supercharging is not so effective as it may appear, and has not been
highly popular, either in large or small engines, but one or two
model engines have incorporated the principle with moderate
success.

In two-stroke engines, the " stepped " displacer piston has
been used in various ways, and separate pistons, operated by
the main or subsidiary cranks, have been used, either in
scavenge blower cylinders or to increase crankcase displacement ; but so far there is little evidence of the general
superiority of engines thus fitted over the orthodox simple
two-stroke, at least in small sizes.

Rotary Blowers

Generally speaking, three types of engine-driven blowers
have been applied for supercharging ; the centrifugal or

"fan" type, the Roots blower, and the sliding vane type. The first of these has been highly successful in very large engines but, as its efficiency depends on both the peripheral velocity of the impeller blades and the mass of the air or mixture passing through them, it is extremely difficult to use it effectively in a small size, and the gearing necessary to drive the impeller at an efficient speed would introduce mechanical complication and inefficiency.

The Roots blower, which may be regarded as a development of the gearwheel pump, has a positive displacement and can be run at much lower speed, so that it can be direct coupled to the engine ; but it is a rather difficult blower to construct in a really efficient form, and suffers from the disadvantage of having to work against the full delivery pressure of the air it displaces.

Sliding-vane blowers have been made in a wide variety of forms, the types mostly used for supercharging having " controlled " or positively-operated vanes to prevent heavy friction due to centrifugal force. All blowers of this class work by positive displacement, so that they will work efficiently at moderate speed and, unlike the Roots blower, are true compressors which only work against back pressure during the effective delivery period of their cycle. A very interesting blower of this type was made some years ago by Mr. Chaddock and used in the experimental work mentioned above. The design follows that of the well-known Zoller supercharger, in which the vanes, four in number, are joined together in opposed pairs and controlled by shoes working on an inner guide ring ; as the tips of the blades do not follow a truly circular path, the bore of the casing must be machined, by generating methods, to a shape which allows them to work at a constant but very fine clearance.

The writer has made some experiments with free-vane blowers, which are much simpler to construct than those with controlled blades, and appear to show some promise of reasonable efficiency, but has not yet applied them successfully to supercharging an engine.

The exhaust turbo-blower has not, so far as is known, yet been applied to model engines, but has been used successfully in full-size practice, though there are many mechanical difficulties in its design. As it takes no mechanical power from the engine, but works on waste pressure, it puts an entirely different aspect on the supercharging problem, and would appear to be applicable to small engines. The exhaust turbine, if properly made and balanced, would be capable of running at the speeds necessary to drive a centrifugal fan efficiently, but problems may arise in designing it in such a way as to avoid trouble by increase of exhaust back pressure. Proposals have been made to drive the blower by a steam turbine, using steam generated by exhaust and cylinder jacket heat, thus cutting out the back pressure problem ; but no practical experiment has been made on these lines, so far as can be ascertained.

Compression-Ignition Engines

Many attempts have been made to produce a really small engine working on the " Diesel " principle ; in other words, an engine in which the fuel (usually of a low grade and high flash point) is injected by a pump and ignited by the heat of compression. Very little success has attended these efforts, by reason of inherent and very formidable difficulties in metering microscopic quantities of fuel, in spraying it sufficiently finely to ignite readily, and in conserving the heat of compression in a very tiny cylinder, so as to produce a high enough temperature to effect ignition of any normal fuel oil.

Of recent years, however, successful engines of the true compression-ignition type have been developed on the Continent, though they are very different to the compression-ignition engines used in full-size practice. They do not employ injection pumps or spray nozzles, but mix the fuel with the air taken into the engine, by means of a simple

" carburettor " practically identical with that employed for small petrol engines. The fuel used must be specially compounded, having among its ingredients an " activator," usually some form of ether or its equivalent, which has the property of a low ignition temperature and a readiness to detonate under compression pressure.

A very high compression ratio is employed, and some provision is usually made for adjusting this ratio while running, either by a " contra-piston " in the head, or by some means of moving the cylinder and head bodily up and down. In this way, some measure of control can be obtained over the point at which ignition takes place, and this serves an equivalent purpose to the " advance and retard " lever of a petrol engine, though it is somewhat doubtful if ignition timing is ever very exact. The cylinder and piston must be made to very high precision limits, as the slightest compression

The " Dyno " 2½ c.c. compression-ignition engine

leak is fatal to the working of the engine. In this respect, engines of this type can hardly be recommended to the amateur constructor, whose facilities for cylinder boring and finishing are not usually adequate for producing the accuracy essential to success with this type of engine. Compression-ignition engines of sizes from about $2\frac{1}{2}$ c.c. upwards have been produced commercially in Switzerland, France, Holland, Germany and Italy, and may be expected to become popular in this country in due course. All those so far encountered are of the two-stroke type, with flat-topped pistons, and long stroke in relation to bore. News has also been received of a somewhat similar engine produced in Sweden, which has an injection pump and spray nozzle as used in full-size practice, but exact details are not yet available.

It is much too early to make definite comparisons between the merits of these engines and those of the more normal internal combustion engine with electric ignition ; but while their utility for certain purposes is beyond question, it would appear that they have very definite limits of power, speed, and flexibility of control ; and being much less suitable for construction, tuning and development at the hands of the amateur enthusiast than the petrol engine, it is believed that the latter will continue to develop and improve for many years yet.

The apparently greater complication of an engine which requires the addition of highly specialised electrical equipment has been proved to be no practical deterrent to its reliability, and in the event of running trouble developing, it as generally easier to diagnose and eliminate than in a superficially more simple engine. Many experienced users of engines prefer the four-stroke to the two-stroke, because its functions are more distinct and straightforward, despite its greater complication ; and on this basis, many will prefer the petrol engine to the compression-ignition engine, even for duties which are equally within the scope of either type. In full-size practice, the "Diesel" engine has many times threatened to supersede the

Another view of the "Dyno" engine

petrol engine, particularly for automobile and aircraft application; but the latter still survives, and moreover, is still the handiest and most convenient source of power yet discovered.

Petrol Turbines

This is another development which, if it arrives at all, is very definitely in the future. Interest has often been expressed by model engineers on the prospect of producing an internal combustion turbine, and the recent developments in full-size practice towards this end have resulted in renewed discussion of the problems involved. There is no doubt that, although some success has been obtained with large I.C. turbines, many of the major problems still remain, and can only be surmounted by long and patient research, to say nothing of the utmost resources of metallurgy and machine-tool equipment. On the strength of some intimate experience with these problems, the

P

writer is of the opinion that they are in many cases inversely proportional to the size of the turbine. One of the greatest difficulties in the functional design of an I.C. turbine is that of compressing the air or mixture prior to ignition, and the best types of rotary compressors leave much to be desired in mechanical efficiency, besides being extremely complex in construction. Combustion chamber and blade cooling would probably be easier in a small engine than a large one, but only at the expense of thermal efficiency.

There is no doubt that a really successful model I.C. turbine would open up new possibilities in reducing the size of engine required for a given power and simplify many of the mechanical problems associated with high-speed reciprocating engines, including balancing and lubrication. But whether it could be produced in a reasonably simple form, suitable for construction by the amateur, and as adaptable to all-round model engin- eering requirements as the present type of engine, are questions which can only be answered by long and patient experiment.

It is far from the writer's intention to damp the enthusiasm of the model engineer who aspires to design and produce new and better types of engines ; on the contrary, progressive thought and action are deserving of every encouragement. But no good purpose can be served by minimising the prob- lems and difficulties which have to be surmounted, or pretend- ing that they do not exist. Many experimenters would cheerfully embark on the conquest of new worlds before they have properly subjugated the old ones. There is ample scope for research and experiment in the very simplest types of engines, and some of the most notable successes in the development and use of model petrol engines have been attained without venturing too far along untrodden paths. A simple engine which works well is better than an " advanced " one that doesn't, and I would exhort the inexperienced reader, before hitching his wagon to a star, to consider the less spectacular but much more reliable possibilities of the humble carthorse.

APPENDIX

CONSTRUCTORS of model petrol engines often find some difficulties in calculating the essential factors in design, especially when it is necessary to produce an engine conforming to pre-determined class restrictions. While these matters are readily dealt with by quite straightforward mathematics, or even simple arithmetic, a good deal of time can be saved, especially in design, if a reference table or other form of ready-reckoning device is available. Some of these problems can be dealt with by alignment charts, or " nomograms," and the two examples reproduced here will cover a very wide range of model petrol engine requirements.

Bore-Stroke-Capacity Calculations

Chart I, which was prepared at the writer's suggestion by Mr. D. H. Chaddock, covers all calculations for bore, stroke and engine capacity, in both English and metric measurements. The method of co-relating the scales in all charts of this nature consists of using a straightedge, or preferably a strip of transparent material with a straight line ruled on the underside, which is laid on the chart, with the line in contact with the known factors on two of the scales ; the unknown factor can then be read off from the position where the line cuts the third scale. For example :—

(1) To determine cylinder capacity, the bore and stroke being known : place the straightedge on the scale at the left to correspond with the bore, and at the right to correspond with the stroke ; capacity is then indicated on the middle scale in either cubic inches or cubic millimetres.

(2) To determine either (a) the bore, knowing the capacity or the stroke, or (b) the stroke, knowing the capacity and the bore : place the straightedge to correspond with the capacity on the middle scale, and with the known factor on either the right or left hand scales ; the unknown factor is then shown on the other scale in inches or millimetres.

(3) To determine bore and stroke, the capacity being known : place the straightedge, as before, on the middle scale at the capacity figure, and see-saw the two ends as required, to find the most suitable dimensions for bore and stroke, taking care to maintain the correct position on the middle scale.

(4) To convert inches to millimetres, or *vice versa* : No straightedge is required in this case, as the figures can be read off directly from either of the side scales.

(5) To convert cubic inches to cubic centimetres or *vice versa* : Proceed as in previous example, but using centre scale.

(6) To determine the total capacity of multi-cylinder engines, the bore and stroke being known : Use the method described in example (1), and multiply by the number of cylinders.

(7) To determine bore and/or stroke of multi-cylinder engines, the total capacity being known : Divide by the number of cylinders, and proceed as in examples (2) or (3).

It will be observed that this chart can not only be used for the conversion of English and metric measurements, as indicated in examples (4) and (5), but is also suitable for dealing with mixed measurements in any order. This is very convenient for most constructors, who commonly use English standards for bore and stroke dimensions of engines which have to conform to metric capacity restrictions.

Power-Speed-Torque Calculations

These arise in cases where it is necessary to assess the ability of an engine of a given power to perform definite types of duty, or conversely, the engine power absorbed in

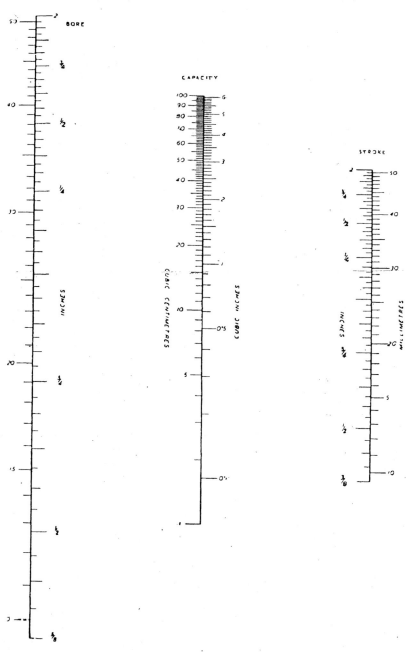

Chart I

www.KnowledgePublications.com

performing a given duty. Chart II has been adapted from a chart prepared to suit full-sized engineering requirements, and originally published in the *Canadian Mining Journal*. In its original form, it was intended to be applied principally to problems of power transmission by flat or vee belt, chain, rope, cable or toothed gearing ; but the principles are applicable to any engineering problem in which the three factors of engine speed, tractive effort, and speed of final drive occur. The chart is, of course, used in exactly the same way as Chart I, by the application of a straightedge to the scales, connecting the known factors of the equation. For example :—

(1) To determine the strength of belt or chain necessary to transmit a given horse-power, when running at a definite speed on a pulley or sprocket of given diameter : Connect the point on the left-hand scale which indicates the pulley diameter with that on the right-hand scale which indicates r.p.m. The result found on the centre scale is then multiplied by the horse-power. Exactly the same method is used to find stresses in gear teeth, or tractive effort exerted by locomotives (or other machines used for traction, haulage or lifting) when the above factors are known.

(2) To determine the speed (in r.p.m.) which can be produced by a given horse-power, when absorbed by a pulley,brake drum or track wheel of given diameter against a known torque resistance or loading : First divide the load (in pounds) by the horse-power to find the required figure on the centre scale ; align this with the figure for pulley diameter on the left-hand scale, and read the result from the right-hand scale.

(3) To find the size of pulley which can be rotated at a given speed, against a known load, by an engine of given power : Proceed as in example (2) to find the figure on the centre scale, but align this with the r.p.m. figure on the right-hand scale and read the result from the left-hand scale.

(4) To find the horse-power measured by a friction brake having a given brake drum diameter when running at a known speed : Connect the figure for brake drum diameter

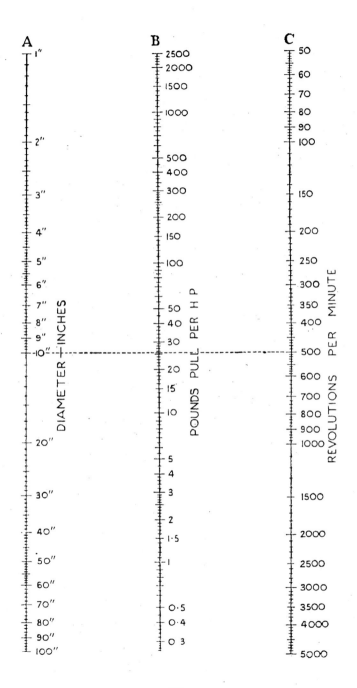

with that of r.p.m., on the left-hand and right-hand scales respectively ; the result on the centre scale is in pounds per horse-power, and must, therefore, be multiplied by the reading on the spring balance or scale pan of the brake to find the power actually exerted. In cases where a steelyard or torque arm is fitted to the brake, the radius at which the load is applied must be multiplied by 2 to find the equivalent of the pulley diameter. With this provision, the method of calculation is applicable to all forms of absorption dynamometers, including electric (swinging field), hydraulic, and torque reaction types.

Silencing

Model petrol engines are often objected to on the grounds that they are inherently noisy ; this is to some extent true of most of the popular types of engines, if they are run with open exhaust pipes, or none at all, and particularly engines which are tuned for high efficiency. Generally speaking, constructors and users of these engines revel in the sound of their exhaust note, and few attempts are ever made at silencing them. It should, however, be noted that the methods which are used for silencing full-sized engines are equally applicable to models, and in engines of moderate performance, at least, there is no reason whatever why they should become a public nuisance for want of some provision in this respect.

Experiments with model petrol engines fitted to model cruising boats, locomotives (including " 1831 "), and used for stationary work, have proved that quite simple forms of silencers, if made of adequate capacity and free from resonance, are highly effective. One of the simplest forms of silencer is an expansion chamber loosely packed with steel wool or machine swarf ; but in engines inclined to run oily or produce soot, frequent changing or cleaning of the packing is necessary.

In high-efficiency engines, some slight loss of performance is almost inevitable when a silencer is fitted, but some modern types of silencers are claimed to cause little or no back pressure, and good results have been obtained with many model power boats fitted with silencers of the Burgess type, in which no baffles are fitted, but the central straight-through pipe is perforated and surrounded by a sound-absorbing packing inside an outer jacket or shell. Silencers of the ejector type, in which air is drawn through the casing to cool the gases and reduce their volume and pressure, have also been used with success.

Two-stroke engines not only have a more aggressive exhaust note than four-strokes, but they are also more susceptible to the effects of back pressure, and in consequence it is rather rare to find them well silenced. One of the most effective silencers yet encountered on this type of engine is that in which water is injected into the expansion chamber, causing rapid condensation of the gases and actually reducing the pressure in the exhaust pipe. This can be quite easily applied to water-cooled boat engines, by leading the discharge from the water jacket into the exhaust chamber, but precautions must be taken to prevent the water spray finding its way back into the engine. The principle is, of course, equally applicable to four-stroke engines.

It should be remembered that the products of combustion of a petrol engine contain a considerable amount of water vapour, and a cold silencer is capable of acting as a condenser until thoroughly warmed through. Engines have sometimes been known to choke and stall through the effect of back pressure caused by water in the silencer. The obvious remedy is to provide means of draining the latter, in cases where it is located in such a way that water can collect. A very small leak will provide a permanent drain, but it should not be too large, and the possibility of it becoming choked should not be overlooked.

Stroke-Bore Ratio

Designers of small petrol engines often find some difficulty in deciding just what relation of stroke to bore should be used for a particular purpose. The older types of engine usually had a long stroke, sometimes as much as twice the bore dimensions, but more modern engines generally have a shorter stroke, " square " engines (i.e. having equal bore and stroke dimensions) being fairly common, and in some cases the stroke is less than the bore.

The most obvious effect of shortening the stroke of an engine is that the piston travels a smaller distance per revolution and thus, for a given r.p.m., the mean piston speed is reduced. It would, therefore, appear that the short-stroke engine is better suited to producing high revolutions than one of longer stroke. In full-size practice, this rule generally holds good, and long-stroke engines are recommended for " slogging " at low or moderate revolutions while short-stroke engines are favoured for purposes where the load is lighter and the r.p.m. higher. This applies also, to some extent, in small engines, but in this case the piston speed is invariably low in relation to r.p.m., and the advantages of the short-stroke engine at high speeds are not so apparent.

There are, however, many other factors which must be taken into account when determining the bore and stroke of an engine. The use of a long crank throw enables the " leverage " on the crankpin to be increased, or in other words, the load on the pin to produce a given crank torque, is reduced. In practice, this is often found to reduce bearing wear on both the crankpin and main journal bearings, and to simplify lubrication problems.

In cases where it is desired to use valves and gas passages of the maximum possible size in the cylinder head, the short-stroke engine provides a greater area of head per displacement volume of the cylinder which is helpful in this respect. On the other hand, a short-stroke engine requires a finer clearance in the head for a given compression ratio, and thus, when it is desired to use a high compression ratio, the shape of combustion head is inefficient, and the internal surface exposed to the flame is large in area, resulting in low thermal efficiency. Long-stroke engines are generally favoured for very high compression, and it is significant that small compression-ignition engines, in which it is necessary to use compression ratios as high as 20 to 1, nearly always have the stroke at least 1½ times the dimensions of the bore.

The leakage path around the piston of a short-stroke engine is greater than that in a long-stroke engine, for a given cylinder capacity, and in cases where differential expansion of the cylinder and piston are encountered greater clearance must be allowed to prevent seizure at high temperatures. Short, large-diameter pistons are more liable to " slap " than those which are long in relation to diameter. Side thrust of the piston against the cylinder walls is much the same in either long or short stroke engines, providing that the length of connecting rod is proportioned to the stroke in all cases ; but that means that the overall length from cylinder head to shaft centre must be greatly increased in the long-stroke engine. Balancing problems are also much the same, regardless of length of stroke, for although the long-stroke piston has farther to travel, it can be made a good deal lighter than one of shorter stroke and greater diameter.

Gas flow, in a long-stroke engine, may have to be faster for a given r.p.m., in cases where valve port diameter is limited, but in two-stroke engines using piston-controlled port admission, the depth of port is in proportion to the length of stroke, so that port area can be maintained irrespective of stroke-bore ratios. Long-stroke engines of this type are generally found easier to scavenge than those having a short stroke.

One outstanding factor which tends to make the short-stroke engine extremely popular, in cases where bulk and weight are highly important, is that its external dimensions can be made much smaller, for a given capacity, than those of a long-stroke engine. This also enables weight per capacity to be reduced, and as makers of commercial engines find this feature to be an important selling point, it is somewhat overdone in these engines at present.

All things considered, it will generally be found that an engine with the stroke slightly greater than the bore gives the most satisfactory service and longest wear ; and where other conditions permit, this type of engine is strongly recommended for such purposes as stationary and general marine work (not excluding racing); and particularly for model aircraft, where moderate speed, high torque and smooth running are called for. Model racing cars, however, owing to the restricted height under the bonnet, often demand extremely short-stroke engines, unless the engines are disposed horizontally or obliquely.

Printed by ELECTRICAL PRESS LTD., Cordwallis Works, Maidenhead, Berks., and published by PERCIVAL MARSHALL & CO. LTD., 23, Great Queen Street, London, W.C.2.

THE "ATOM MINOR" MARK III

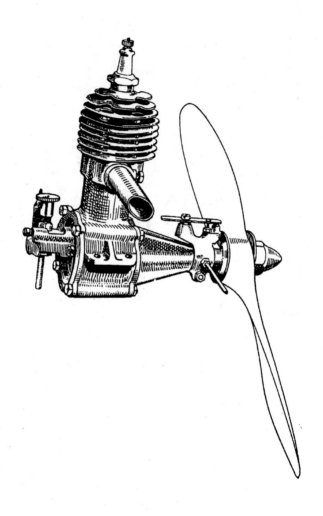

THE
"ATOM MINOR"
MARK III
6 c.c. ENGINE

By

EDGAR T. WESTBURY

Atom Minor was originally designed in 1933.
Reprinted 1984 © TEE Publishing 0 905100 56 5

www.KnowledgePublications.com

PREFACE

THIS modest little booklet has been produced to meet the many requests for detailed instruction on the actual construction of a typical model petrol engine, to supplement the details already available in the shape of blue prints and general information on the design of these engines. While the usefulness of the latter is beyond question, and is quite sufficient for the needs of the constructor who has had some practical experience with the subject, the beginner who approaches the task of constructing an engine for the first time may need further guidance on the methods and procedure in machining and fitting the components ; which, it is hoped, the following pages will provide.

The particular engine dealt with is not only a thoroughly sound and successful one, and moreover, a highly suitable subject for the amateur constructor with limited equipment, but it also entails operations which are fairly typical of general practice in the construction of such engines, so that the information given is applicable to the construction of engines of other types or sizes than that described. Limitations, not only of equipment, but also in the supply of materials, are a serious problem to many amateur constructors, and this has also been given special consideration by arranging for the use of readily available materials wherever possible, and alternatives or substitutes for special metals which are often specified for engine construction.

THE
"ATOM MINOR"
MARK III

MOST constructors of power-driven model aircraft in recent years have been more or less content to rely upon ready-made engines, but during the war, when such engines have been practically impossible to obtain, an increasing number of constructors have been turning their thoughts towards the possibility of producing their own engines. While welcoming this tendency, I would point out that the construction of one's own engine should not be regarded as a mere stop-gap expedient to tide over a temporary shortage in the supply of the commercial article, but that it is a very desirable object in itself. There are many reasons why model aircraft enthusiasts should take a keen and practical interest in the inner secrets of the design and construction of the engines used for propelling their machines ; not only does it enhance the interest and educational value of model aircraft, but it is also conducive to progress in aerodynamical design and development.

Although, in the manufacture of full-sized aircraft, it is customary to make airframes and engines in separate factories, or in separate departments of the same factory, their design is very closely inter-related, and no designer in either branch who is intent on efficiency and progress can possibly afford to disregard the other. The power requirements of model aircraft may not be so exacting as those encountered in full-size practice, but there is still a very strong case for a closer liaison between the two branches of design than has hitherto been obtained.

Many aircraft constructors have been deterred from attempting engine construction by the lack of facilities for mechanical engineering work. It is, of course, inevitable that the construction of an engine involves much more elaborate tool equipment than that of the airframe, including the use

1

of a metal-turning lathe, not necessarily of an expensive or elaborate type, but capable of carrying out fairly accurate work. But this extension of the model aircraft constructor's workshop is more than justified for its own sake, and many parts of the models, apart from the engines, can be produced much more efficiently by the use of such equipment than is possible with the primitive tool kit which is often deemed sufficient for building airframes. I wish it were possible for me to tell readers how to build petrol engines without the use of a lathe, but the fact remains that it is generally impracticable if not absolutely impossible, to do so ; I may mention, however, that most of my own engines were built with the aid of a lathe which only cost £5 when I bought it brand new !

During many years of experience in the construction of model petrol engines, I have sought not only to produce designs for engines which were efficient, and well suited to their intended purpose, but also capable of being constructed with limited equipment, and requiring no exceptional skill on the part of constructors. Most of these engines have been highly successful, though they have often been criticised in comparison with some of the more popular commercial engines, mostly on account of their weight. But the line I have taken in engine design has always been dictated by sound reason, and I claim that the types of engines which I have recommended for amateur constructors are more suitable for their specific purposes than the orthodox commercial light-weight engine designs.

This point is often imperfectly appreciated, and I am often called upon to explain why a home-made engine should be any different in design to one produced in a factory. The first and most evident reason is that the equipment used to produce the two types of engines is totally different. Not only is the amateur's equipment of a simple type in most cases, but it is often limited to only one machine tool—the lathe—on which all machining operations have to be carried out. In the quantity production of engines, on the other hand, consider-able elaboration of equipment, including the use of special jigs and fixtures, and special-purpose machines for such operations as milling, grinding and honing, may be justified if production be expedited thereby.

It is also necessary, or at least very desirable, that the design for the home-produced engine should be adaptable, to enable slight variations from the original design to be incorporated, either for experimental purposes, or to suit the fancy or special requirements of individual constructors. This is more important than it may appear at first sight, and I have found that it is more the exception than the rule for engines to be built exactly to the blueprints. A design which is too rigid, permitting of little or no variation in any of its parts, is in my experience unlikely to become popular among constructors.

This adaptability must extend also to the materials used in construction, and it is generally necessary to allow for the use of common and easily-obtainable materials in the design. The designer of a commercially-produced engine may specify the use of a special alloy-steel for heavily-stressed engine parts, such as the crankshaft or cylinder ; but if any such material is specified for an engine intended for amateur construction, every other prospective builder is sure to ask whether some other kind of steel will not do just as well ! Many constructors are very keen on making use of material already available, and I have had to take into account the possibility that engine parts may be made up from old lorry axles, re-melted motor-car castings, railings, and even sash weights ! Robustness in the inherent design of an engine is absolutely essential when one cannot be absolutely certain of the

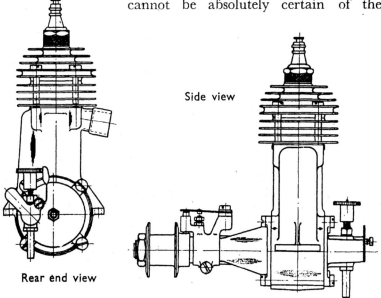

Side view

Rear end view

quality of the material which is to be put into it. An engine design can always be pared down to reduce its weight, but whether any really useful purpose can be served by doing so is quite another matter, and it is my opinion that this policy has been very much overdone in the past, both in certain types of commercial and home-produced engines.

In producing an engine design to suit the requirements of the up-to-date model aircraft constructor, I have borne all these points very carefully in mind ; and another consideration which is equally important is the matter of engine size. It is possible to build a successful petrol engine of very small capacity, if one exercises sufficient care and skill, but it cannot be denied that the smaller sizes of engines below 4 or 5 c.c., however well designed and made, have a lower useful performance, and are more temperamental than those of more liberal capacity. Again relying on the lessons of past experience, I have come to the conclusion that for facility of construction and all-round usefulness, an engine of about 6 c.c. has strong claims to popularity. It can be built quite successfully on a lathe of the type and size commonly found in model engineering workshops, and is not so small as to involve " watchmaking " or super-precision work in its components ; it can be made practically free from " temperament," and will propel a plane large enough to be aerodynamically efficient without being so bulky as to be unwieldy in construction or handling.

Plan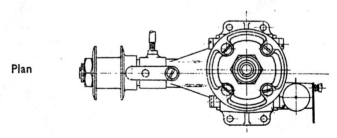

The "Atom Minor" Mark III Engine

The design which I am describing is one which has been evolved from a long series of experiments, beginning with the original "Atom Minor," which was produced expressly to suit Colonel Bowden's requirements in 1932. This engine was of 15 c.c. capacity, and it is hardly necessary to recount details of its pioneer successes ; but the need

The "Atom Minor" Mark III engine as originally
constructed, with carburettor at the front

for a smaller engine was soon evident, and within about
three years I had produced a smaller version of the design.
which was known as the " New Atom Minor," and ha? a
capacity of 6.3 c.c. ($\frac{3}{4}$ in. bore by $\frac{7}{8}$ in. stroke). By the time
this design was tested out and ready to turn loose on con-
structors, however, the commercial model aircraft engine had
arrived, and had diverted attention from the possibilities of
amateur construction of engines, which has never since been
very popular in this particular field. Examples of the smaller
engine have, however, been produced by many amateurs, and
have proved very successful in model aircraft and power boats.
    During the war, one of these engines was used in model
aircraft experiments by one of the Services, and produced

Later development of the engine, with carburettor shifted
to the rear end

some initial results which justified the development of the
design for further research work. This resulted in the production of the "Atom Minor" Mark III engine, a rather
more efficient and adaptable engine than its predecessor. A
number of these engines have been produced by a well-known
firm of engine manufacturers, and have proved not only
highly satisfactory and reliable in performance, but much
more durable and capable of sustaining rough usage than
most engines of this class. One of the first engines made, after
four years' hard work, is still a consistently easy starter, and
shows no perceptible wear of the bearings, cylinder or piston.
An engine of this type, with small detail modifications, such
as a high-compression piston and cylinder head, has been

tuned up by Mr. J. Cruickshank, of model racing-car fame, and has produced 0.29 h.p. at a speed of 11,000 r.p.m. These details are given to show that the design is one that has been fully proved, and may be recommended with confidence to the amateur constructor.

Specification

Most of the original constructional features of the " Atom Minor " 15-c.c. and 6.3-c.c. engines have been retained, but one noticeable difference is that the orthodox port admission system used in these engines has been superseded by a rotary admission valve of the type which has proved highly successful in the " Kestrel " 5-c.c. and several other larger engines. The built-in full reservoir of the 6.3-c.c. " Atom Minor " (also used in the " Kestrel ") has not been incorporated in the present design, though it can be added if desired ; its omission is intended to eliminate possible restriction in the adaptability of the engine. This motive has also been the guiding principle in other features of design, including the carburettor, which, although built into the crankcase, like that of the " Kestrel," has a reversible jet assembly which enables the engine to be installed either in the upright or inverted position without structural alteration.

As originally constructed, the carburettor and admission valve were situated in the front of the engine, on the main bearing housing, but while this gave satisfactory results, the controls were rather crowded—especially as the contact-breaker was also mounted on this housing—and their location in close proximity to the airscrew made manipulation somewhat risky. The design was therefore modified by arranging the admission valve and carburettor on the rear crankcase endplate, so that the air intake is at the back of the engine. This is more convenient for most model aircraft installations, but there is some advantage in the forward-end carburettor for certain purposes.

Optional Sizes

Another modification which has been made in the later development of the engine is a slight reduction in the bore diameter of the cylinder, to bring the capacity within the 6 c.c. limit. This is a purely optional feature, and where it is not necessary to conform to any class restriction of engine capacity, constructors may prefer to retain the original cylinder bore of

¾ in., in order to obtain the maximum power output with little or no perceptible increase in the bulk or weight of the engine. The dimensions which will be given for the cylinder and piston will, however, conform to the smaller bore, so that the engine may truly be described as within the 6-c.c. class.

The general arrangement drawings show the external appearance of the engine, and in describing the various details, I shall try to indicate the reason for their particular features of design, and point out what modifications of shape, dimensions or materials are permissible without defeating their essential objects.

Readers who propose to construct this engine may be assured that castings and materials of approved quality will be available, and that any technical difficulties which they may encounter, as a result of inexperience in this particular class of work, will be given careful consideration. I am aiming to promote " engine-consciousness " among model aircraft enthusiasts, and shall spare no pains in assisting anyone who is making an attempt to produce an engine for himself.

Most of the structure of this engine consists of light alloy castings, which are reasonably straightforward in design, and easy to machine on a light lathe of the type popular among model engineers. The main body casting comprises the barrel of the crankcase and a vertical extension surrounding the cylinder skirt, and the only absolutely essential machining operations on it are the boring and facing of these parts, which must be truly at right-angles to each other. Other machining operations, the accuracy of which do not vitally affect the engine performance, are the boring and facing of the exhaust socket, the planing or milling of the underside of the bearer feet, and drilling and tapping of holes.

One thing which I would like to impress upon constructors is that, although it is very important to work accurately to dimensions in machining engine components, a still more important consideration is the *geometric* accuracy of these parts, that is to say, alignment, squareness, parallelism, etc. Adherence to correct dimensions, such as the diameter of a shaft or a bearing bush, is very desirable, because it very much simplifies the machining and fitting of mating parts ; but it matters very little in the construction of a single engine whether a shaft, or even a piston, is one- or two-thousandths of an inch too large or too small, so long as the bearing, or the cylinder bore, is machined to suit. The manufacture of engines in quantity, where parts have to be completely interchangeable, is quite another matter, and in this case it is necessary to specify the limits of error which can be tolerated in the machining of each part. I have sometimes been criticised for not specifying limits on my engine drawings ; but the fact is that comparatively few of the constructors of these engines have the means of measuring to such fine limits.

While insisting on the need for accurate workmanship in the construction of any type of model petrol engine, I trust that readers will not be deterred, either by limitation of equipment, or lack of confidence in their own ability, from attempting this work. Accuracy in machining or fitting is mainly a matter of taking pains, not only in the actual work, but in practising to acquite delicacy of touch, and cultivating the habit of thinking in exact terms. The question of ways and means, although by no means unimportant, is really a secondary matter, and good work can be done with the simplest equipment ; this applies not only to machine tools and workshop appliances, as already discussed, but also to measuring instruments. By all means avail yourself of the advantages of fine measuring instruments if you can ; the use of a micrometer for outside dimensions is strongly recommended as a valuable aid to accuracy—but do not get the idea that a formidable array of expensive gauging equipment is essential before you can begin building an engine.

MACHINING THE CASTINGS

In order to ensure that the vertical and horizontal bores of the body casting are truly at right-angles, the use of an angle-plate for mounting the casting on the lathe faceplate is recommended. Some constructors are rather scared at the task of setting up work in the lathe, especially when angle-plates or similar fixtures are involved ; but actually there is no simpler way of ensuring true squareness, which is most essential to the efficient working of any engine. The angle-plate used does not need to be an elaborate one—I have used one improvised from the side girder of an old bedstead before now—but it is most essential that it should be true, which can easily be checked up when it is mounted on the faceplate, by means of a small engineer's try-square. This precaution should not be neglected, even when using a ready-made angle-plate, as these are not always above suspicion. In the

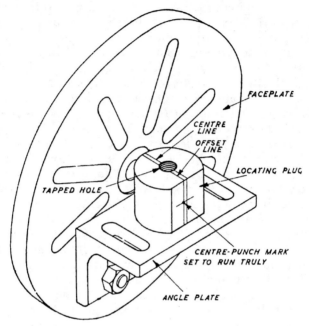

Locating plug set up for ensuring correct setting of body casting to bore cylinder seating

case of a home-made angle-plate, some filing and scraping are usually necessary to true up the surfaces, and I do not propose to describe this process in detail, as it consists of elementary fitting work, some knowledge of which must be acquired by every constructor before attempting any serious work on engine building. It will also be necessary to drill some holes in both faces of the plate, in convenient positions, for the purposes of clamping.

Boring the Crankcase Casting

It is recommended that the horizontal bore of the crankcase should be machined first. There are at least two sound methods of setting the casting up in the lathe for this operation ; one is to hold it in the four-jaw chuck, and the other to mount it by the bearer-feet on packing-blocks mounted on an angle-plate, which in turn is clamped to the lathe faceplate. The former method sounds the less formidable, and will perhaps be favoured, but it involves risks of error unless due precautions are taken. It will be necessary to reverse one of the chuck-jaws to grip over the edge of the top flange, the opposite one bearing on the underside of the crankcase, and the other two over the edges of the bearers. The latter should do most of the holding, but it is unnecessary, and most undesirable, to use heavy pressure in chucking such a light casting, as it is very easily distorted out of shape, or even crushed, by the exercise of brute force on the chuck-key.

The front face of the casting should be set outwards ; but here the question arises—which *is* the front ? It will be noted that the body casting is reversible, so that the exhaust port may be either on the right- or left-hand side ; the object of this is that the engine can be arranged to run *with equal efficiency* in either an anti-clockwise or a clockwise direction. On account of its particular design, the " Atom Minor " is not capable of running *efficiently* in either direction without certain structural alterations, including the reversal (from front to back) of the main body. Nearly all model aircraft engines run in an anti-clockwise direction, looking from the airscrew end ; and if this procedure is to be adopted, the exhaust port should be on the left, when looking at the main bearing-housing face of the casting. It is, of course, practicable to reverse the casting after it has been machined, provided both faces of the crankcase barrel are machined parallel and square with the cylinder axis.

If the second method of setting up the casting is adopted, the underside surfaces of the bearers should be trued up (though not necessarily finished) by filing or otherwise, so as to be square with the vertical axis. This may be checked by laying the casting down on a flat plate, with a packing wedge under the top flange, so that it is truly horizontal, and applying a try-square to the undersides of the bearer-feet. If desired, the holes in the latter may be drilled to assist in attaching them to the packing-blocks, which may be of metal or hardwood ; in either case, they should be of equal thickness and dead parallel.

The actual setting-up, whatever method of mounting is adopted, follows ordinary lathe work practice, and need not be described in detail. Readers who do not understand this work are advised to obtain some elementary instruction, or to study a good practical handbook, such as " The Beginner's Guide to the Lathe," or " Practical Lessons in Metal Turning " (both obtainable from the publishers, Percival Marshall Ltd.). It may, however, be desirable to point out that in setting up castings, which may not be perfectly accurate on all surfaces,

Body-casting

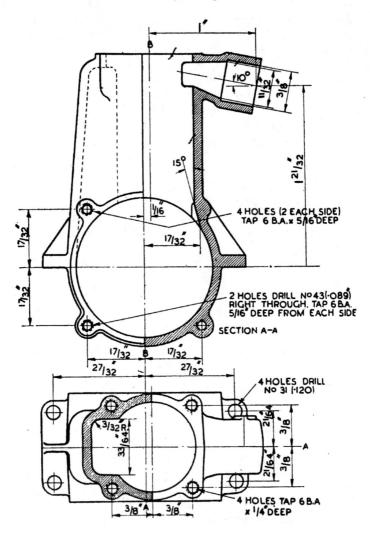

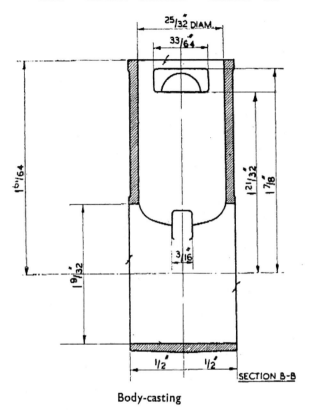

Body-casting

reference should always be taken from the portions which are finally left unmachined—in this case, the *outside* surface of the crankcase. Unless this is done, the crankcase walls will not be of even thickness when the inside is bored.

Setting Up

Setting-up is always far more tedious than actual machining on these small castings, but should on no account be shirked, especially on this particular casting, as the entire success of the engine will depend upon its accuracy. Boring and facing are very simple operations, carried out at the same setting, the front face being cut back till the tool just skims the upper extension of the casting. It is not impracticable to face the rear side at the same setting if the chuck-jaw on the underside is packed out by a block of wood or metal so that the tool (a deep internal recessing or undercutting tool) will clear it when facing right to the edge of the bolting-lugs ; but it is the usual practice to carry this out in a second operation with the casting mounted on a mandrel with the reverse side outwards. The mandrel may be made from any convenient piece of metal, or even hard wood, the only consideration being that it should fit the bore fairly tightly and run truly, either in the chuck or between centres.

Machining the Vertical Bore

It has already been stated that the essential requirement of locating the bore for the cylinder-skirt exactly at right-angles to the shaft axis can be assured by mounting the casting on an angle-plate clamped to the lathe faceplate. There is, however, another important requirement in setting up the casting for this operation ; namely, the correct location of the bore in the side plane, relative to the shaft axis. Reference to the end view of the casting will show that the cylinder-axis is offset from the crank-axis by $\frac{1}{16}$ in. ; this is perhaps a rather unusual feature in model two-stroke engines, but one which I have adopted on several of my engines for very sound reasons.

It would be rather difficult to ensure locating the casting on the angle-plate by the usual means, as the orthodox methods of marking-out are cumbersome and, in my experience, not very reliable when dealing with small castings. I have generally found it best to use some form of simple mounting-jig which locates the casting from a previously machined reference surface, for operations of this nature.

In the present case the jig consists of nothing more elaborate than a cylindrical plug turned to fit neatly in the crankcase-barrel, and slightly less in width than the distance between its joint faces—say about $\frac{15}{16}$ in. This has a tapped hole through the centre, and a flat cut on one side to produce a face about $\frac{7}{8}$ in. wide. A centre-line, square with this flat, is marked on the plug with a scribing-block, both on the end face and across the flat. Another line, $\frac{1}{16}$ in. to the side of the centre-line, is then similarly marked.

Clamping

After clamping the angle-plate roughly in place on the lathe faceplate, the plug is secured to the angle-plate by a set-screw from the underside. It is desirable to place a paper washer, larger in diameter than the plug, underneath it, to improve the grip, and also to protect the machined face of the casting when it is clamped down. The set-screw used for securing the plug may be either a short one, extending not more than halfway through the plug, or a long one extending beyond the plug far enough to fit a nut for clamping down the casting. The essential thing is that the plug must be capable of being secured independently of the casting, so that it can be set up in its correct location before the latter is mounted.

Before finally tightening the set-screw, the plug should be set so that the parallel marks on its face are dead square with the faceplate, the flat face being at the front, and the offset line to the left of the centre-line. A line is then scribed across the flat face, parallel with the surface of the angle-plate and $\frac{1}{2}$ in. (that is, half the crankcase width) away from it. The point where this line intersects the offset line is then carefully marked with a centre-punch, as shown in the explanatory drawing.

Having secured the locating plug firmly in its correct position, the angle-plate is now adjusted bodily on the faceplate to bring the punch mark dead central with the lathe axis, using a scribing block or other means to assist accurate setting, after which the bolts securing the angle-plate to the faceplate are tightened up. It is desirable to balance the assembly, by clamping any odd pieces of metal on the faceplate, opposite the angle-plate, so that the lathe will run without vibration. The casting is then slipped over the plug, front crankcase face downwards (i.e. exhaust socket to the left) and clamped down with a plate or " strap "—not forgetting the paper washer—secured by the central set-screw, or better still, by a long strap with bolts at either end passing through the side slots of the angle-plate. It will be found necessary to set the outer end of the casting sideways so that it runs truly—this is done by swinging it round the plug, not by shifting the angle-plate—and it will be seen that this method of setting-up positively ensures that the axis of the bore will be in its correct location.

The boring and facing operation is now quite straightforward and will take much less time than the setting-up. Some constructors may begrudge the time taken in making clamping devices or simple jigs, but attempts to find short cuts are liable to lead to dangerous pitfalls. Any device which assists or ensures accuracy in engine construction is worth while.

Showing how the crankcase barrel may be bored and faced, holding the casting lightly in the four-jaw chuck with one jaw reversed

The distance of the upper surface of the casting from the centre of the crankcase is of great importance, as it influences the position of the piston at the end of the stroke, and therefore affects port timing. Measurement should be taken from the crankcase centre and may be marked out on the edge of the casting before setting it up on the angle-plate. Should any error be made in this dimension, however, it may be compensated for when making other components, *so long as it is recognised and duly noted.*

Exhaust Socket

The exact angle and location of the socket are not vitally important, but it is just as easy to do the job properly as otherwise, and while the casting is mounted on the faceplate, it may be swung round 100 deg. and the angle-plate readjusted to bring the port to central for boring and facing. A bevel gauge or protractor, set to 80 deg. and presented to the cylinder seating face of the casting, will enable the required angle to be obtained. Another way to bore the socket would be to clamp the casting on the lathe cross-slide at the appropriate angle and use a drill in the lathe chuck, but this is little, if any, easier and less accurate.

Only the outer bore, to take the exhaust pipe, can be machined, the rest of the passage being cored so as to blend with a rectangular slot on the inner face. This may be cleaned out and faired off with riffler files or rotary cutters. The size of exhaust pipe specified ($\frac{3}{8}$ in. diameter) is adequate to carry the gases in a normal aircraft engine of this capacity, but, if desired, the socket may be opened out or tapped to take a $\frac{7}{16}$ in. diameter pipe ; this is recommended in cases where the engine is to be tuned up for maximum performance. The engine will, of course, run quite well without an exhaust pipe, but I think the fitting of the pipe is well worth while, and one of my pet aversions is the open-exhaust engine which sprays sooty oil all over the fuselage of a nice clean 'plane.

The feet of the bearers may be finished by milling, if one possesses the necessary facilities, such as a vertical slide or milling attachment ; but, if not, they may be filed. It is very desirable that they should be in exact alignment, and level with the shaft axis, as this very much assists in setting the thrust line accurately when installing an engine. Most users of engines nowadays prefer to mount them on bearers, but there is a great deal to be said in favour of bulkhead mounting, which can be carried out quite easily in this engine, by attaching the rear crankcase cover flange to a mounting ring or plate. If this plan is adopted, the bearer flanges on the engine may be cut away.

Drilling and tapping operations for the crankcase and cylinder fixing-screws are best left until the mating components are completed, so that their location can be matched with the clearance holes in the latter.

It will be observed from the drawing of the body casting that a small internal notch, $\frac{3}{16}$ in. wide, is cut at an angle of 15 degrees to the vertical, at the base of the cylinder skirt, where it joins the crankcase barrel. The object of this, of course, is to clear the connecting-rod at its point of maximum angularity. This notch may be produced by filing, and its exact size and angle are not of great importance, so long as the required clearance is provided ; but it should always be remembered that clearances anywhere in the crankcase should never be unnecessarily large, or pumping efficiency will be impaired.

Any cleaning-up operations on the outside of the casting which may be considered desirable may be carried out at this stage, except the matching up of the bolting lugs with those on the flanges of front and rear covers, which should be left until the latter can be temporarily fitted in their correct positions. It may be mentioned that steps are being taken to ensure that the castings which are supplied for building this engine are of the highest possible quality and finish, so that little or no cleaning up will be required.

I have considered it desirable to describe in detail the operations on this casting, as I find that many engine constructors encounter difficulties through incorrect machining procedure. The other castings involve no special problems in setting-up and machining.

MAIN BEARING HOUSING

The casting for the main bearing housing may be machined in two or three different ways, the essential thing being to ensure that the register spigot of the flange, the central hole, and the turned seating for the contact-breaker are all concentrically true with each other. One of the best and safest methods is to bore the central hole first and then mount the casting on a true-running mandrel, between centres, for the remaining operations. The casting may be held in the three jaw chuck, gripping it over the register spigot, for drilling ; but first the surface of the spigot should be examined to see that it is free from rough lumps which might throw the casting badly out of truth when held in this way. Before fully tightening the chuck, the nose end of the casting should be set to run as truly as possible by tapping it gently with a mallet, using a piece of chalk, held in the fingers with the hand steadied against the tool post, to check the accuracy while running the lathe at high speed. If the nose is out of truth, the chalk will touch the high spot and indicate where it should be tapped to correct the error.

After tightening the chuck, a light facing cut should be taken over the end of the nose, and it should then be centred by means of a centre-drill held in the tailstock. It is most

Boring the upper extension of the casting, which is mounted on an angle-plate (note sheet of paper under it to avoid marring the machined surface), and located by the plug as previously described

important that the centre should be exactly true, and in this respect, holding the centre-drill in a tailstock drill chuck does not always provide sufficient rigidity to avoid wobble. A much better method of holding the centre-drill is to turn a short piece of steel to fit the tailstock socket, and bore it centrally a push fit for the drill, which may be secured by a grub screw. If the centre-drilling is not absolutely true, it is hopeless to expect that the drilled hole will be true either ; in fact, the error will multiply in proportion to the depth of hole drilled.

Do not attempt to drill the hole to its full size, or reamering size, right away, but start with a " pilot " hole, using a drill about $\frac{3}{16}$ in. diameter, which should be keen and well backed off. Run the work at high speed, and do not force the pace of feeding the drill, backing it out frequently to clear the chips. With due care, a perfectly true hole right through the casting should be produced, and may be followed by one or more larger drills to open up the bore to 19/64 in. diameter, finishing with $\frac{5}{16}$-in. parallel reamer, held in the tailstock chuck, and

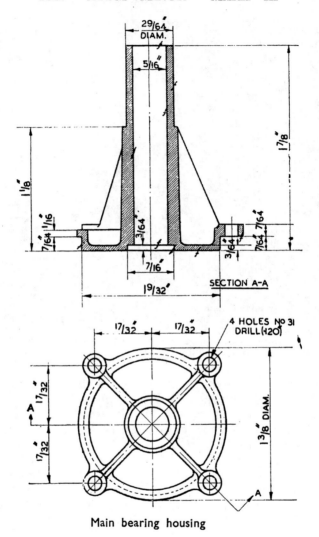

Main bearing housing

fed by pushing the tailstock bodily along the bed of the lathe, running the spindle slowly or turning it by hand. A lubricant is generally desirable for reamering aluminium, thin soluble oil or paraffin being suitable, and frequent backing out of the reamer will avoid clogging.

Next centre a piece of $\frac{3}{8}$-in. mild-steel bar about $2\frac{1}{2}$ in. long, and turn it between centres to form a mounting mandrel, which should be very slightly tapered—not more than 1 or 2 thousandths of an inch in the length of the work—and fitted so that it can be pressed in fairly tightly. A dead smooth file may be used to finish the mandrel to size. When the work is thus mounted, it may be run between centres to turn the back face of the housing, the spigot and flange face, then reversed to turn the contact-breaker seating.

The endwise dimensions should be taken from the unmachined front face of the flange ; if this should be found to run slightly out of truth, take the measurement of $\frac{1}{16}$ in., shown on the detail drawing, as representing the thinnest point. Great care should be taken to fit the spigot to the crankcase barrel, as a well-fitted spigot counts for a good deal in the structural strength of the engine, relieving the crankcase studs of practically all stress. A sharp-angled right-hand side tool may be used for all the operations on the outside of the housing. While set-up for turning the contact-breaker seating, the tool may be used to skim the projecting faces of the bosses on the front of the flange.

Incidentally, a hammer should not be used in fitting or removing the mandrel ; in the absence of a mandrel press, the vice may be used, supplemented by pieces of tubing or odd bushes to act as distance pieces.

The recess in the flange end of the bore can best be formed by fitting the work on a stub mandrel held in the chuck, using a small boring tool. It is not absolutely essential that this recess should fit snugly over the rim of the bush, and, if desired, it may be made slightly oversize to provide a clearance ; but the depth shown should be adhered to fairly closely.

After ascertaining that the bosses on the housing flange correspond fairly closely with those on the crankcase when the parts are assembled (note that there are four alternative positions), the stud holes may be marked out and drilled, keeping them all on the same pitch circle and as equidistant as possible. The tapping holes in the crankcase may then be " spotted " or jigged from these holes. It will be desirable to mark the position of the housing relative to the crankcase for guidance in subsequent assembly.

Rear Endplate

The projection of the carburettor boss from the back of the endplate makes it a little more difficult to set up than the front housing. It is intended to be held over the rim in the four-jaw chuck for machining the spigot and the inner face, but it has been found that some of the chucks used on small lathes have very shallow jaws, which will not accommodate the depth of the carburettor boss. In such cases it may be necessary to make a temporary "accommodation chuck" by turning an old bush, or other suitable piece of scrap, with a recess to fit over the bolt lugs of the casting, and having a large enough clearance hole to allow the carburettor boss to pass through. To ensure that the outside surfaces of the lugs are concentric, they may be skimmed up, holding the work by the spigot, before fitting to the recess, into which it should press sufficiently tightly to hold during the turning operations.

These are generally similar to those on the housing flange, and the same tool may be used, similar care being exercised in fitting the spigot. It will be seen that this is a good deal longer than that of the front housing (the object being to avoid unnecessary crankcase clearance), and a part of the surface is relieved so as to make assembly easier than would be the case if the full length were a tight fit. The centre hole should be drilled and tapped while set up in the lathe, and should be truly central, using the centre-drill as before to locate the drill correctly. Hold the spigot in the three-jaw chuck for skimming the faces of the bolt-holes and the centre boss.

The hole which forms the carburettor passage may be drilled in a drilling machine if desired, but a better plan is to mount the work in the lathe, running eccentrically, and bore it out. As the small size of the job makes it difficult to secure to the lathe faceplate in the ordinary way, it may be clamped to a small disc of any convenient material, held in the reversed jaws of the four-jaw chuck. A recess may first be turned in the disc to fit the spigot of the end-plate, which can then be held quite firmly by a single clamp or strap, bearing on its centre boss with a packing piece in between. The radial and angular position of the bore should be marked out on the end face of the carburettor boss, and the disc set over until this runs truly.

Centre the boss fairly deeply and drill through to 15/64 in. diameter, then taper out the end of the hole with a reamer or D-bit, if available, or by means of a small boring tool. The exact angle of taper is not highly important, but it works out to an included angle of 15 degrees at the intake end and

$7\frac{1}{2}$ degrees at the discharge end. It is quite a simple matter to make D-bits from $\frac{5}{16}$-in. silver-steel rod for carrying out jobs of this nature ; the rod is first turned to the angle required, then filed away to exactly half its diameter, hardened and tempered. These tools cut very cleanly, and without chatter, being, in many cases, preferable to reamers for occasional jobs.

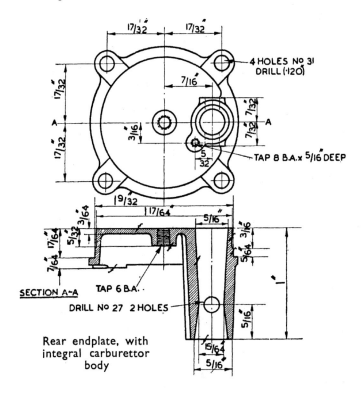

SECTION A-A   TAP 6 B.A.

DRILL No 27 2 HOLES

Rear endplate, with
integral carburettor
body

The taper at the discharge end of the bore can be finished by holding the D-bit in the lathe chuck and supporting the casting against the tailstock barrel. Run the lathe at moderate speed, and feed the tailstock up very cautiously to avoid any tendency to snatch.

Marking-out and drilling the bolt-holes is carried out in the same way as for the front housing, and they can similarly be used to locate the tapping holes in the crankcase, but in this case there is only one possible position for the endplate ; that is, with the carburettor horizontally to the side of the centre-line, on the same side as the transfer passage, whichever direction of engine rotation is selected.

The flat inner face of the end plate forms the seating of the rotary admission valve, and must be perfectly smooth and true. It may be finished by lapping on a piece of plate-glass, but this process may be left until the valve is ready to be fitted, when both parts may be lapped and mated before final assembly.

CYLINDER HEAD

This component may be produced by turning all over from aluminium alloy bar. After facing the end, it is centred and drilled through to 21/64 in. diameter to tap out for the plug then counterbored for the combustion chamber and recessed to fit the cylinder spigot. A round-nosed boring tool should be used for roughing out the shape of the combustion chamber followed by a hand tool, similar to a round-nosed scraper, for finishing. A form tool may be made if desired, but when used on a small lathe it will be found rather prone to chatter, and will not usually give such a clean result as a hand tool.

Before turning the cylinder-head cooling fins it is a good policy to drill and counterbore the holes for the holding-down screws, as if this operation is left till afterwards, there will be a tendency for the drill to run out of truth as it passes through the fins. It will be seen that the counterbore passes through three fins, and is finished flush with the surface of the thickened fin which serves as a bolting flange. The best tool for counter-boring, or at least for finishing the flat face, is a spot-facing cutter or "pin drill," and if a ready-made one is not available, this also may be made from silver-steel rod.

To form the fins, a parting-tool $\frac{1}{16}$ in. wide should first be used to cut grooves almost to finished depth, after which a finishing tool 3/32 in. wide, with a rounded nose, is used to clean up the sides and bottom of each groove. The tips of the fins are rounded off with a smooth file.

Taps to cut the thread for the sparking plug are available from most tool shops, but screw-cutting in the lathe is not a

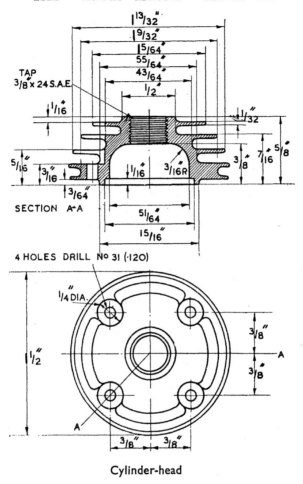

Cylinder-head

difficult operation. The top face of the plug boss should be faced cleanly and dead square with the thread.

Cylinder Barrel

This is the most important single component in the engine in respect of accuracy, and every possible care must be taken in machining it. The material recommended, for constructors who wish to avoid the necessity of carburising or other heat-treatment of the bore, is fine-grained cast-iron, preferably die-cast or centrifugally cast in solid or hollow bar form. Should steel be used, it should be either a high-tensile alloy steel, which will be found very difficult to machine, or a mild-steel may be used, which will machine fairly easily, but is not sufficiently hard to produce a really durable surface in the bore unless it is carburised. It is true that many engines have been made with mild-steel cylinders, but their working life is comparatively short, especially when used with ringless pistons which have no accommodation for wear ; and the least fault in lubrication may lead to serious trouble.

Assuming that mild-steel is used for the cylinder, it is recommended that the treatment applied is such that only the bore is hardened or toughened to resist wear. This may be done by first machining a blank to the dimensions shown in the lower part of the drawing, and carburising it by packing in a closed iron box filled with case-hardening composition, heating the box to a red heat and maintaining this temperature for about an hour. If the usual box as employed for this purpose is not available, it is possible to dispense with it by simply making two large discs or washers to close the ends of the bore, with a bolt to go through the centre and keep them in place ; then pack the bore of the cylinder with the case-hardening powder, close up, and heat up the blank as directed above. The blank should be allowed to cool naturally, and the outside is then machined to its finished dimensions, except for this, which will remove the carburised " case," leaving the steel in its original soft condition.

If means are available for internally grinding the cylinder, it may be re-heated and quenched out, so as to leave the bore surface glass-hard, which is the nearest approach to the ideal for long wear. But hardening almost invariably introduces some distortion, which is extremely difficult to correct by any other means than grinding, and few amateurs have facilities for carrying out this work. It should also be noted that the material removed by grinding must be allowed for, by leaving the bore about 0.010 in. under size in the initial machining.

The carburised surface, if left unhardened, is a good deal more resistant to wear than untreated mild-steel, and it will be fairly satisfactory to leave it in this condition, finishing the bore surface by lapping with abrasive paste on a soft metal (lead or copper) lap. In this case, no more than about 0.001 in. need be removed in the finishing process, providing that the bore is left as smooth and parallel as possible in machining.

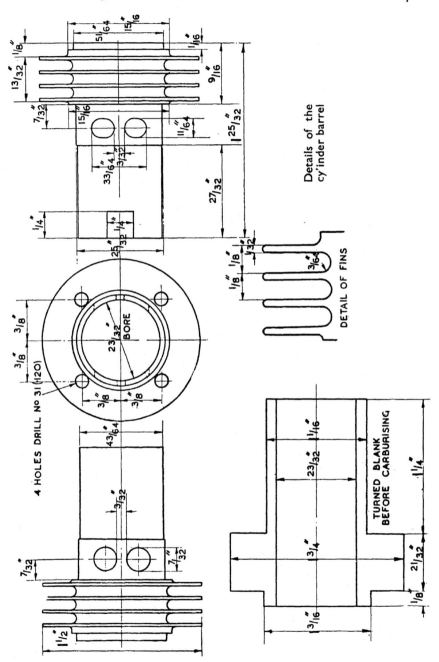

Details of the cylinder barrel

DETAIL OF FINS

BORE

4 HOLES DRILL No 31 (·120)

TURNED BLANK BEFORE CARBURISING

The process of lapping cannot be described here in detail, but it has been dealt with many times in practical articles in *The Model Engineer*, and is also described in the " M.E." handbook " Grinding, Lapping and Honing." It is emphasised that lapping is something more than a mere polishing process, and that mere " finish," as such, is not the most important thing to aim at. Correct methods in lapping will produce accuracy to the very finest possible limits, but it calls for care and patience, and results cannot be obtained by rush tactics.

If cast iron is used for the cylinder, the processes employed are generally the same, including lapping, but with the exception of heat-treatment. The cast-iron cylinder barrel will be rather fragile when finished, and will need careful handling. It may be noted that the lower end of the cylinder skirt, which is shown as 1/64 in. smaller in diameter than the port belt, need, in fact, only be reduced in size just sufficient to slide easily into the crankcase, if it is desired to keep this part as strong as possible. The port belt should be a tight " wringing " fit in the crankcase, so that leakage of air from the crankcase to the exhaust port is avoided.

Before turning the fins, the holes for the cylinder bolts should be drilled, following through from the holes in the cylinder head. The cylinder should be mounted on a mandrel for turning the fins and other final machining of the exterior. It will be seen that the fins are formed similarly to those of the cylinder head, and it may be mentioned that this is not the ideal shape of fin for producing the most effective cooling, but is better than a square-bottomed fin, and will be found generally adequate for a model aircraft engine. If, however, it should be proposed to use the engine in an enclosed position, or for any purpose where the flow of air past it is reduced, a tapered form of cooling fin, both on the cylinder barrel and the head, will be found better.

The cylinder ports are formed by drilled holes, the positions of which are plainly shown on the drawing. It will be seen that the ports on the transfer side are slightly elongated with a file after drilling. It is permissible to join up the ports to form a single slot, both on the transfer and exhaust sides, which will increase the port area considerably, but this will show very little, if any, advantage at the speeds required for aircraft propulsion, and will reduce the bearing area of the cylinder wall. If a piston fitted with rings is employed, slotting out in this way is not permissible, as it would result in trapping and breaking the rings.

A notch $\frac{1}{4}$ in. wide by $\frac{1}{4}$ in. deep is filed in the base of the skirt on the transfer port side, to clear the connecting-rod at its point of maximum angularity. After this work is completed, it will be found desirable to give the cylinder a final lapping, to remove burrs and possible distortion caused in cutting the ports.

THE PISTON

The piston may be made either of cast iron or suitably treated steel. Aluminium pistons have been tried out in these engines, but owing to their high coefficient of expansion, these need to be fitted with a large clearance, which tends to make engine starting difficult, unless they are equipped with piston rings. Cast-iron pistons generally give the most satisfactory service in small engines, and their greater weight compared with aluminium pistons, makes very little difference at normal running speed. A piece of cast-iron " stick " may be used for machining the piston from the solid—it is hardly practicable to cast it to the finished shape internally—and an ample extra length should be allowed for holding it in the chuck. If the external surface is rough, it should first be turned all over to produce a true cylindrical surface for holding in the chuck.

The recommended procedure in machining the piston, as detailed in the drawing on page 30, is perhaps, a little unorthodox, but has been arrived at as the result of a good deal of experience in machining pistons from the solid. It avoids many of the difficulties which commonly arise in the machining operations, and facilitates accuracy in the finished product.

Turn the outside of the piston to within about 1/32 in. of finished size, and beyond the main cylindrical portion, the size may be reduced to form the sides of the deflector, but this should be left attached to the chucking piece. Next drill the centre, to a depth of $\frac{15}{16}$ in., with a $\frac{3}{8}$-in. drill, finishing the end of the hole with a flat cutter or end-mill. Bore out the mouth of the hole, to a depth of 31/64 in., to 21/32 in. diameter, and undercut the inner end of the hole with an internal recessing tool, to 19/32 in. diameter, for a width of 11/64 in., leaving a " land " or internal collar 9/32 in. wide to form the gudgeon-pin bosses.

The position of the gudgeon-pin is now marked off on the outside of the piston, using a point tool to mark the circumferential line $\frac{5}{8}$ in. from the end, and setting a scribing block on the lathe bed to mark cross lines exactly across the centre of the diameter. The inter-sections of these lines should be carefully centre-punched, and drilled from either side with a small drill, after which they are opened out to reamering size

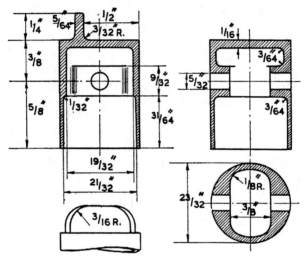

Piston and gudgeon-pin details

(No. 24 drill) and reamered 5/32 in. diameter. It is most important that the gudgeon-pin should be quite square with the axis of the piston ; a very slight divergence from the exact centre of the piston diameter is not a serious fault.

The slotting out of the inside of the piston to form the gudgeon-pin bosses is intended to be done by circular milling, but this may be difficult for readers who have no milling appliances available. A very close approximation to the shape shown in the drawings can, however, be produced without anything more elaborate than a simple vee packing block to hold the piston on the cross slide of the lathe, and a $\frac{3}{8}$-in. end-mill in the chuck. The vee block should be packed up so that the piston is exactly at the level of the lathe centre, and its axis is also dead in line with them. Position the gudgeon-pin holes exactly vertically by inserting a length of 5/32-in. rod in them, and sighting against a square held on the lathe bed. It is necessary to clamp the piston down firmly on the vee block, and the reason for keeping it on the chucking piece will be evident, as the piston itself would be much too fragile to hold in this way. Adjust the cross slide to take a light cut on the side of the hole, and feed the saddle backwards and forwards each time a cut is applied, until the slot is about 19/32 in. wide, or a little more, the idea being to remove as much superfluous metal as possible.

Replace the piston in the lathe chuck and set it up to run truly for finishing the outside. It should not be turned to fit in the cylinder bore, but left on the tight side (about 0.001 in. oversize) and then lapped with a ring lap to a " squeaking fit," after which a final finishing with very fine abrasive, such as jewellers' rouge or metal polish, will produce a highly-polished and wear-resisting finish. As the exact clearance cannot be measured by any simple means, there is little point in quoting it, but the piston should just be capable of being

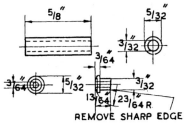

Gudgeon-pin and end pads

pushed through the cylinder bore by hand, and no tight or loose spots should be apparent. All traces of abrasive should be removed from both piston and cylinder by prolonged soaking in paraffin, syringing out holes and crevices, and wiping with a clean rag.

The piston is now parted or sawn off from the chucking piece, and held in a wooden clamp (made by boring a hole in a piece of hardwood and sawing it in half) for shaping the deflector, which may be done by sawing and filing. Note that there is a slight radius at the root of the deflector to assist heat conduction, and the entire surface of the piston which is exposed to flame should be smoothly finished to retard the deposition of carbon. The deflector of this piston is higher than usual in these small engines, with the idea of ensuring good scavenging under all conditions, but should it be found desirable, for any reason, to increase the compression ratio, as when using special fuels, a high deflector would foul the cylinder head, and it would have to be reduced in height. On no account should the deflector touch the cylinder wall at the sides.

Gudgeon-pin

This is simply a hollow mild-steel spindle, fitted fairly tightly to the piston bosses and case-hardened. Soft pads or ferrules of brass or aluminium are driven into the ends, so that in the event of the pin moving endwise, it cannot score the walls of the cylinder.

Connecting-rod

A cast bronze rod has been found to give good results in this engine, but some difficulty has been experienced in obtaining sound, reliable castings in this size, and if there is the least doubt on this point, there is a risk of wrecking the engine by a connecting-rod breakage. On the whole, a rod machined from solid bronze or duralumin, preferably the latter, on account of its lighter weight, will be found safer. If a steel rod is used, the eyes will have to be bronze bushed. The machining of connecting-rods has been described several times in *The Model Engineer*, but it may be stated that, in any kind of rod, the point of vital importance is the exact parallel alignment of the two eyes, which may be assured in various ways. Perhaps the simplest is to clamp the cast or rough-formed rod to a flat plate, taking care not to bend or distort it in doing so, and set up the plate on the faceplate of the lathe, so as to bring each of the eyes in turn into the central position for drilling and boring to size. The rest of the work on the rod may be carried out by any convenient method, so long as it does not involve straining the rod out of shape, and the fluting at the sides of the rod is not absolutely essential, though it is desirable in order to reduce weight as much as possible. It will be seen that one end of the big-end bearing is internally chamfered or flared to clear the internal radius or " fillet " on the crankpin, where it joins the crank web. This bearing should be a normal working fit, the gudgeon-pin being a little tighter. Do not forget to drill the oil holes in the ends of the rod, to admit oil mist *at the point of lowest pressure*.

In the home construction of engines, slight errors of dimensions of the various parts may produce a cumulative discrepancy affecting the position of the piston in the cylinder, and therefore the port timing. To avoid any trouble from this

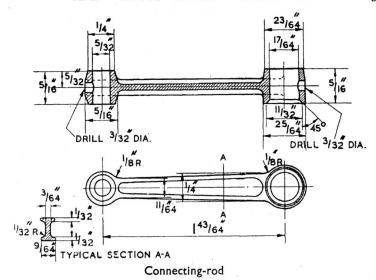

Connecting-rod

cause, it is my invariable practice to check up by using a temporary or " dummy " connecting-rod, made by drilling two holes in an odd strip of material, before making the permanent rod. The piston should just uncover the exhaust port fully at bottom dead centre ; if the trial with the dummy rod shows that it travels too far down, or not far enough, the difference can be noted, and the distance between the bearings altered to suit when making the rod. Other ways of correcting the discrepancy have been referred to.

CRANKSHAFT

The most essential point about the machining of the crankshaft is that the main journal and the crankpin should be truly parallel all ways. Accuracy of dimensions is also important, particularly in the throw of the crankpin, and the diameter of both shafts ; but errors in these respects are capable of being compensated by suitable treatment of other parts. If, however, the crankpin is out of true parallel alignment with the main shaft, there is no cure, and the engine can only be made to run by allowing an abnormal amount of clearance in the crankpin bearing, which results in poor mechanical efficiency, with hammering and rapid wear of the working parts involved.

A series of articles dealing with the methods of constructing crankshafts has been published in *The Model Engineer*, and it is recommended that these articles should be studied by anyone approaching work of this nature for the first time. Some appalling mistakes in method have been made by inexperienced constructors, but if the job is tackled properly, there is nothing formidable about making a crankshaft.

It may be noted·that the crankshaft of this engine is very robust in design, including a rather thick web ; and the object of this is to cope with eventualities in the methods of construction or materials which may be employed. The shaft may be made either by machining from the solid, or fabricated by brazing ; the former method is recommended as most suitable for the average constructor. Not that there is anything unsound about a properly brazed-up shaft, but it is liable to entail more time and trouble, and involve more risk of error than a shaft made from the solid ; moreover, there is some danger that if carbon or alloy steels are used in construction, the heating may affect their strength and render them inferior to the commonest mild steel.

Successful crankshafts have been made by screwing the main journal and crankpin into the web, and preventing them from moving afterwards by riveting over or sweating with soft solder. This method, however, is not recommended, because of the risk of inaccuracy in producing both the internal and external threads ; and assuming even the slightest error in this respect, there are obviously no less than *four* potential sources of inaccuracy in a simple overhung crankshaft of this type. Taking all things into consideration, it is just as easy, and much safer, to machine the shaft from the solid ; it enables one to use either a high-tensile steel (which can be used in the untreated condition, to provide maximum strength and toughness, or quenched to provide hardness), or a low-tensile mild steel, which can be surface hardened if desired. All these variations have been successfully tried out in the " Atom Minor " Mark III engine.

For the benefit of those readers who cannot obtain access to the articles referred to, it may be briefly mentioned that of the various ways of machining crankshafts, one may choose between methods which need no special fixtures or appliances but call for special care in setting out, and methods which dispense with marking out, but rely upon the use of eccentric chucking fixtures such as a Keats vee angle plate. Of the two courses, I prefer the latter, because when once made, it ensures positive accuracy every time ; but for dealing with only one crankshaft, the former method may be considered quicker and less troublesome.

To mark out a bar for machining a crankshaft, it should be laid in a pair of vee blocks on a surface plate, and a scribing block, with the scriber point adjusted to the centre height of the bar, used to mark off a centre line on each end of it. The bar is now turned 90 degrees, so that the centre line is vertical, as verified by checking against a square on the surface plate. Another centre line is marked in this position, and then, after checking the height of the scriber point from the surface plate, it is raised by an amount equal to the crank throw, and another line scribed on each end of the bar. Care must, of course, be taken in all cases to see that the bar does not shift while marking off these lines ; if a clamp is fitted to the vee blocks, it should be used to prevent this eventuality.

The intersections of the lines should be carefully marked with a fine centre-punch, and followed up by centre-drilling. As the centre of the main journal at the crankpin end will be cut away in facing back the web, a small hole should be drilled sufficiently deeply to ensure that this centre is retained ; but great care should be exercised to see that it runs truly in line with the centre at the other end of the bar.

The crankshaft can now be turned between centres, setting it first on the eccentric centres for turning the crankpin, and then on the main centres for turning the main journal. Both should be finished smooth and parallel, and if any trouble occurs in producing the required finish and accuracy, they may be lapped with a soft metal ring lap while still set up for turning. The use of a file and emery cloth to correct errors in this respect is not highly desirable.

Sawing and filing may be resorted to in shaping the sides of the crank web, but if the crank is turned with the aid of an eccentric chucking fixture, this may also be utilised to enable these surfaces to be machined with a boring tool, by setting the main journal about $1\frac{1}{16}$ in. off centre and adjusting it rotationally to cut away the web in the right places. The exact shape of the web is, of course, unimportant, so long as it produces an effective form of balance weight, substantially similar to that shown here.

A $\frac{1}{8}$-in. hole should be drilled through the centre of the crankpin to take the driving pin of the rotary valve. With care, this can be done by ordinary drilling methods, following on from the drilled centre ; but it is better still, if the shaft can be set up in the lathe on the crankpin centre, and this is one of the points which demonstrates the advantage of a fixture for chucking the shaft eccentrically, thereby enabling the turning and drilling of the shaft to be done at one setting.

Propeller Hub

This is machined from solid mild steel at one setting, including the tapered bore, which can be formed either with a taper reamer or a boring tool, but in any case should be left as true and smooth as possible. The exact angle of taper is not important, provided that the collet is made to fit properly. Before parting off the hub, the cam surface on the back rim may be formed by setting it up eccentrically (here again, a vee angle plate may be found very useful) and turning away a part of the circumference, as shown. It is desirable, but not absolutely essential, to case-harden the hub when finished.

The hub washer may be parted off from 1-in. steel or duralumin bar, after facing, chamfering and drilling the end, and if a correctly set parting tool is used, it will need little or no machining on the back face.

Mild steel is used for the hub collet, which can also be machined all over at one setting. After facing and centre-drilling the end, it is drilled to $\frac{1}{4}$ in. reamering size, taking great care to keep the hole truly concentric and then finished with a reamer or D-bit to a fairly tight push fit on the crankshaft. The end is then turned down to $\frac{3}{8}$ in. diameter and screwcut to take the hub nut, which should not be a coarser thread than 24 t.p.i., as the section of metal is somewhat thin to take the tension of the nut at this point ; the nearest British Standard thread is $\frac{3}{8}$ in. $\times$ 26 t.p.i., as indicated on the drawing.

Next the taper is turned on the collet to mate with the internal taper of the hub. It is most important that this should fit the latter all along its length, and if any difficulty is encountered in machining it to the required accuracy of angle, a smooth file may be used for final fitting. Use marking colour to test the fit of the collet in the hub, and adjust the size so that there is about $\frac{1}{16}$ in. of " draw " allowed for pulling up the collet when assembling the hub on the shaft.

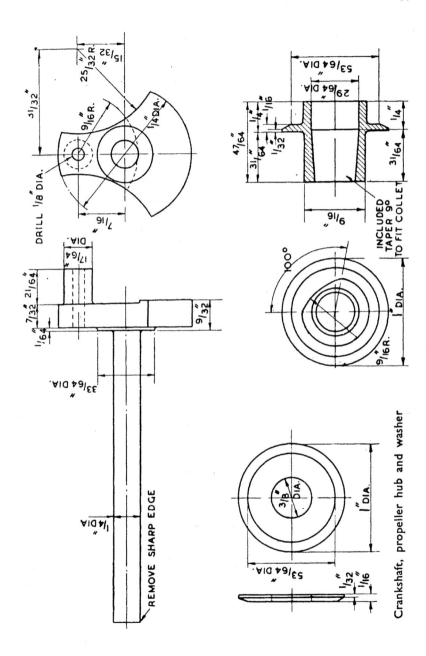

Crankshaft, propeller hub and washer

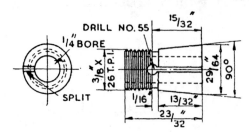

Hub collet detail

Some constructors find difficulty in obtaining a secure grip with taper fits of this kind, but the fault lies, not with the method, but with their execution of the work. There are many practical advantages in fitting the hub by friction grip, as distinct from a positive drive by a square or flat on the shaft, which is quite common in small engines, but is liable to result in shaft breakage in the result of a crash landing.

Constructors can best assure success with this method of fitting by exercising care and patience in machining, and avoiding " short cuts," such as attempting to machine internal and external tapers at one setting of the lathe slide rest. These methods may appear at first sight to be infallible, but experience soon proves the contrary, and many failures have resulted by blind reliance on them. Another point is that it is impossible to lap or " grind in " taper fittings, as a means of correcting a poor fit, though a mere touch to finish the surfaces is permissible.

The collet is shown split on one side only, but it is permissible to split both sides, and this will be found easier if equipment is limited. By drilling a hole as shown at the end of the sawcut, the flexibility of the collet is improved. Remove all burrs, both inside and out, before assembling this component, which should not be hardened.

The bracket for the contact-breaker consists of an aluminium casting, the main machining operation on which is the boring of the centre hole and facing front and back. It can be set up in the four-jaw chuck, taking care that the circular portion of the outside runs fairly truly ; the front side is then faced and centred, then drilled undersize and opened out with a boring tool to a tight push-fit over the end of the main bearing housing. To face the other end, the bracket may be mounted on a pin mandrel.

The rest of the work on the contact-breaker is mostly drilling and tapping. If a drilling machine is available, the casting may be mounted in a small vice or clamped against the side of an angle plate by a bolt through the centre. The hole for the push rod should have the bore left as smooth as possible, and the use of a small reamer or D-bit is recommended for this purpose. Drill the hole for the clamping screw before splitting the bottom lug ; it will be seen that one side of the hole is tapped and the other opened out to clearing size. The tapped hole in the side lug is intended to take the screwed end of the rod, also shown in the same drawing, which serves as the control lever for advancing or retarding the ignition timing. This may either be fitted to screw in stiffly or have a lock nut for tightening it ; the form of the control rod is optional, and may be varied to suit requirements.

A contact screw and rivet, with tungsten tips, will be available, and it is probable that the spring blade with rivet fitted will also be supplied ; however, it may be mentioned that the spring is a fairly stiff one, about 0.020 in. thick, which may be made from a clock or gramophone spring. The insuating bushes may be turned from hard vulcanised fibre or bakelite, and the push rod made from the same material. Note that the terminal tag for the attachment of the L.T. lead

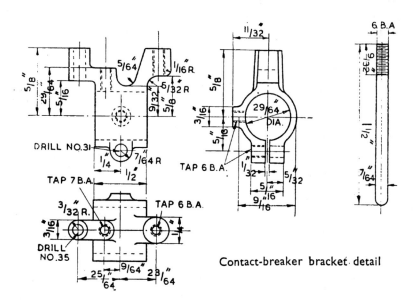

Contact-breaker bracket detail

should be placed between the spring and the top insulating bush, as it must be insulated from the bracket and the holding-down screw.

The spring should be given a slight downward "set" so that it makes firm contact between the points when free. On assembly, the contact screw should be adjusted so that the clearance between the points is about 0.005 in the open position. The clamp screw of the bracket should be adjusted so that it will move fairly stiffly on the bearing housing ; as the bracket can move right round the full circle, it may be timed to work in any position, but it is best to keep the control rod more or less horizontal and the spring blade uppermost, whether the engine is run upright or inverted.

CARBURETTOR

The component which calls for most skill, or at least most care, in machining is the jet tube, which should be made of tough brass—not the soft " screw rod " which is so often used for mass production of small components. Hexagonal material is preferred, but if this is not available, round rod will serve, if flats are afterwards filed on the collar to enable it to be held while screwing up the top nut. Hold the rod in the chuck for turning the top end, including the drilling of the central hole, with a No. 52 drill to a depth of 25/32 in. Great care should be taken to start this hole dead truly, with the aid of a centre

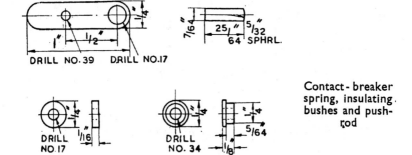

DRILL NO. 39   DRILL NO. 17

7/64"   25/64"   5/32" SPHRL.

DRILL NO. 17   1/16"

DRILL NO. 34   1/8"   5/64"

Contact-breaker spring, insulating bushes and push-rod

drill, and the lathe should be run at high speed for efficient action of the drill, the feed of which should not be forced. In deep drilling, frequent backing-out of the drill is advisable to avoid choking with swarf. The thread on the outside of the tube (No. 4 B.A.) should be cut with a tailstock die-holder to ensure that it is truly axial and concentric, after which the component is removed from the chuck, and a simple chucking fixture is made to hold it in the reverse position, by drilling and tapping a 4-B.A. hole concentrically in a short piece of odd material held in the chuck. It is advisable to counterbore this hole 9/64 in. diameter to allow the tube to screw right home to the base collar, thus providing the maximum rigidity for turning the lower extension and drilling the centre. Taking the same precautions as with the hole at the other end, it is centred and drilled to a depth of $\frac{9}{16}$ in. with a No. 52 drill, after which the jet orifice is drilled with a No. 70 drill, held in a small pin chuck and applied *by hand* with the lathe running at the highest possible speed. If a No. 70 drill is not available, a small spear-point drill, made from a sewing needle by flattening the two sides on an oilstone and producing cutting edges at about 90 degrees on the end in the same manner, will serve this purpose. The exact size of the hole is not highly important, as the jet orifice is adjusted by means of the needle. A cross hole, which also is not critical in size, is drilled in such a position that it comes in the centre of the air passage when assembled.

It will be observed that the cross hole for the jet tube in the extension of the rear endplate is drilled to clearance size for the tube, and this is necessary if it is desired to be able to insert the tube from either side, in order to adapt the engine for

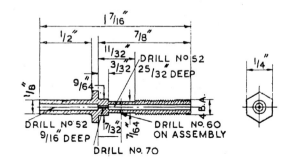

Details of jet-tube

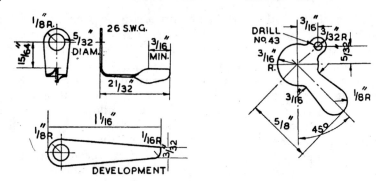

Air shutter and check spring

either upright or inverted running. But if it is to be permanently used in one or the other position, it is a good policy to tap one side of the hole so that the jet tube can then be screwed in, and the top nut is then only required to lock it in position. The tension stress is then taken on the threaded part of the tube, and not on the reduced neck below the thread.

It may be observed that the base of the jet tube, which is shown plain, for the attachment of a fuel pipe by soldering, or by the use of a sleeve of petrol-resisting synthetic rubber, may be modified to take a screwed union, or one of the " banjo " type, if desired. The original engine of this type has a " banjo " union, fitting over the outside of the extension, which is cross drilled to form a passage way, and the end is screwed to take a blind nut, which holds the banjo in place and also forms a closure at the lower end. Removal of this nut allows the jet tube to be cleared or sediment to be readily drained away.

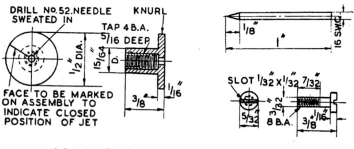

Adjusting head   Air-shutter retaining screw

The adjusting head for the jet needle is a simple job which calls only for normal care in drilling and tapping concentrically, and turning the outside and the upper rim at the same setting. It is made in brass, and the edge is knurled or serrated to provide a hold for the check spring. After temporarily assembling the jet tube in place, the adjusting head is screwed on to within about one thread of its full depth, and the jet needle, made from a piece of 16-gauge steel or nickel-silver wire, with a fine point turned on the end, is pushed into the jet tube as far as it will go, and sweated into the adjusting head.

The check spring, made from spring steel or phosphor bronze, and the air shutter, from steel, bronze or duralumin sheet, are simple jobs which call for no special comment. An 8-B.A. steel screw, with a plain portion under the head, forms the pivot of the air shutter, and a spring washer or a short, stiff spring, is interposed under the head to form a friction check.

The rotary valve may be cut from steel plate, the most suitable material being the grade of carbon steel known as gauge plate, which has a ground surface, and may generally be relied upon for true flatness ; but ordinary mild-steel plate may be used, providing that it is initially flat and is not distorted in cutting out or in subsequent handling. Within limits, the thinner the disc is the better, but as very thin metal may be difficult to true up, and liable to distortion when riveting in the driving pin, it is not advisable to make it much thinner than $\frac{1}{16}$ in., as shown on the drawings. After cutting the plate roughly to shape, it may be trued up on the edge by clamping it against the faced end of a piece of bar held in the chuck, using a $\frac{1}{8}$-in. screw through the centre hole to hold it in place. The angles of the cutaway sector should be checked by means of a protractor, or by some form of indexing gear in the lathe.

It is most important that the radial position of the pin should be correct, so that it will engage the crankpin freely, without introducing any tendency to force the valve off its seat ; one of the most important factors in the success of the rotary valve is that it should " float " freely with no constraint whatever from the crankshaft. The simplest way to ensure this is to make a simple drilling jig, by drilling and reamering a hole in a piece of steel, to take the main journal of the crankshaft, countersinking it slightly so that the crank disc will rest against it. Clamp the shaft temporarily in place, and run a $\frac{1}{8}$-in. drill down through the hole in the crankpin to " spot " its position on the steel plate. Next remove the crank-shaft, and make a spigoted plug to fit the hole in the plate, with a hole tapped to take a $\frac{1}{8}$-in. screw in its centre. This is used to attach the rotary-valve disc to the plate, after which a 3/32-in. or No. 42 drill is used to follow through from the marked position on the plate. The drilling should, of course, be carried out with a reasonably accurate drilling machine, or against a tailstock pad in the lathe to ensure that it is square with the surface of the plate ; and in locating the position of the valve disc, the angular position of the cutaway section should be properly adjusted. Countersink the driving-pin hole on the working face side, and rivet in the pin, which is turned from mild steel, the shank being an easy fit in the hole, and well rounded or chamfered on the end to facilitate engagement with the crankpin on assembly. Take care not to distort the plate in riveting, and file the projecting part of the pin dead flush with the surface of plate.

The working surface of the plate is finally lapped on a piece of plate glass with fine carborundum paste, until it shows an even matt surface all over. Similar treatment should be applied to the seating face on the crankcase endplate, but in this case, a more mild abrasive, such as brick-dust, should be used, and great care taken to remove all traces of it afterwards.

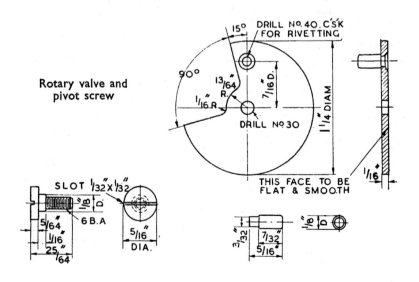

Rotary valve and pivot screw

Should it be desired to run the engine at very high r.p.m., balancing of the rotary-valve disc is desirable, and this may be carried out by riveting a piece of 1/32-in. plate near the lower edge of the cutaway, checking the balance in the usual way, by mounting the disc on a mandrel and rolling it on knife edges. This treatment is not necessary for engines running at working speeds not exceeding 6,000 r.p.m.

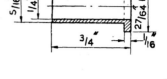

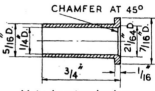

CHAMFER AT 45°

Main bearing bushes

The pivot pin on which the valve disc runs is turned from mild steel and case-hardened. Note that the plain part under the head is a working fit in the centre hole in the disc, and its length should be such that when screwed fully home, the head of the screw will clamp the disc against its seating. Slacken it back just sufficiently to allow the disc to rotate freely, and lock the screw by means of a nut on the outside of the endplate.

It should be noted that the drawing of the rotary valve shows the working face side, arranged for anti-clockwise engine rotation. Should it be desired to run the engine in the opposite direction, reverse the valve from left to right—which may be done by simply putting the pin in from the other side —and also reverse the endplate to bring the carburettor on the right instead of the left, looking from the rear end. It should also be observed that the main body is also reversible, as previously explained.

Main Bearing Bushes

These should be turned from a medium-hard bronze or gunmetal, and if length allows, may be machined all over at one setting and parted off. If only short pieces are available, drill and reamer the bores first, and mount them on a mandrel for turning the outside. It will be seen that the two bushes are identical except that the inner one is slightly countersunk at the flange end to clear the fillet of the crankshaft journal. The outside diameter of the bushes should be about 1/1,000 in. larger than the holes, with a slight taper on the end to assist entry, and should be pressed home in a mandrel press, or the vice will serve if no press is available. As the bores will contract slightly, a reamer should be passed through the bushes after insertion, to clean them up finally, and ensure a smooth working fit for the shaft.

No oil grooves are necessary in the bushes for engines of normal duty. The bearing surface they provide is much greater than that in most commercial engines, and they will have a very long working life if properly fitted in the first place. After four years of really hard work, the original engine of this type shows no perceptible bearing wear.

Cylinder Ports

This operation has purposely been left till last, because it will give an opportunity for a final check on all essential dimensions, and allowance for any possible errors which may arise. The engine should be temporarily assembled, and rotated to ascertain that all moving parts are working freely. It is possible that the connecting-rod may be fouling either the crank web, the rotary-valve pivot screw, or the cylinder skirt, and may need easing slightly on the sides or edges ; but if the discrepancy is very great, there is obviously something radically wrong with the setting out or machining of the parts. The rod may possibly bind sideways through incorrect end location of the crankshaft, or insufficient end float between the gudgeon-pin bosses ; these errors can be corrected by machining away the side faces of the rod eyes, or the flange of the inner main bush. Assuming, however, that the working parts are all in order, the crank should be put on bottom dead centre, and the position of the piston checked ; if this is found to be correct, the ports may be drilled in the positions indicated in the detail drawings of the cylinder barrel ; but should there be any discrepancy, the reason for this should be sought, and, if possible, corrected before proceeding further. The effect of slight errors here and there have already been referred to, including the influence of the connecting-rod length, and in my experience, these errors are rather the rule than the exception. But should it be found difficult or impossible to correct them, the ports in the cylinder may be drilled in such a position as to ensure their correct timing, which is one of the most essential factors in the success of any two-stroke engine. The port positions should be such that the exhaust ports are fully uncovered at bottom dead centre.

The reason why drilled ports are specified in this engine is because many novices appear to lack confidence in their ability to mill or file ports in the correct place, or of the correct size, and it is generally simpler to mark out and centre-punch a position for a drilled hole. But if the constructor prefers to do so, slots may be formed instead of round holes, and will have the effect of providing greater port areas, giving a much snappier exhaust note, though making little difference to performance at normal working speeds. The exhaust ports should in any case be elongated sideways a little, as seen in the cylinder details. Should piston rings be used in the engine, wide port slots are impracticable, and round or squared-out holes or ports, sufficiently narrow to prevent the rings being trapped, are essential.

Slight errors in port timing rarely prevent an engine from working, though they have far-reaching effects on performance. It is better to err on the small side, if anything, as it is much easier to open up a port than to make it smaller. After cutting the ports, all internal burrs should be carefully removed with a half-round scraper, and the cylinder bore lightly lapped with a fine abrasive, to remove possible high spots, before re-assembly.

ASSEMBLING THE ENGINE

Little comment on this is necessary, as the position of the various parts is fairly clear from the drawing, and no hand fitting should be involved if they are properly machined. But do not neglect the obvious points, such as putting the piston the right way round, that is, with the deflector nearest to the transfer-port side. The contact-breaker, hub collet and cam are best assembled before attaching the front housing to the crankcase, as this permits of holding the crank web firmly in the vice (using soft clamps or packing to avoid marking it), while screwing up the hub nut. The latter should first be tightened just sufficiently to enable the hub to be turned stiffly with the fingers to facilitate setting the contact-breaker timing. Set the control lever in its normal working position, as considered suitable and convenient for the way in which the engine is to be installed, and with the crankpin 30 degrees before top dead centre in the direction of rotation, set the cam so that the points are just breaking ; then fully tighten the hub nut, taking care that the hub does not shift. It may be found desirable to hold the hub with a pair of gas-pliers during this operation, interposing a strip of thin leather in the jaws to prevent marking the hub. After the assembly has once been pulled up tightly, the hub nut may be removed for fitting the airscrew or flywheel, without relaxing the grip of the hub collet.

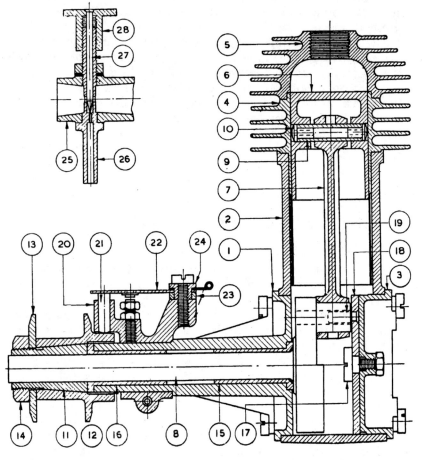

Sectional assembly drawing of engine

The components of the " Atom Minor " Mark III engine before assembly

To remove the hub at any time, it is advisable to make an extractor to hook over the flange, and with a hollow screw to bear on the end of the hub collet ; this will be found to work much more expeditiously and easily than by the use of brute force, which may distort the hub and burr up the threads of the collet.

The airscrew boss will be held quite firmly between the hub flange and the washer, without the need for spikes or serrations which are often provided on commercial engines, and not uncommonly serve the purpose of tearing up the boss of the airscrew more effectively than anything else. It is much better to avoid too positive a drive to the airscrew ; as already explained, the ability to slip under excessive torque may be very useful in a crash landing.

No packing of any kind should be necessary in the joints of the engine, beyond a smear of shellac varnish or similar preparation on the joint faces. Steel screws should be used for holding the parts together ; the cylinder holding-down screws should preferably have threads only long enough to screw properly home, though such screws may be difficult to obtain, and may have to be specially made. If this is done, they may with advantage be made with hexagonal heads, and distance collars under the heads, raising them sufficiently to project above the cylinder-head fins, so that a spanner can be comfortably applied.

The fuel tank used with this engine may be of any convenient type, and situated in any convenient place. A metal fuel pipe is strongly recommended, though a sleeve of petrol-resisting rubber may be used as a connector. The fuel recommended for this engine is ordinary petrol, as used for motor vehicles, with the admixture of a fairly heavy oil, such as Castrol XL, in the ratio of one part oil to four of petrol ; with this fuel, about three-quarters to one turn of the jet screw, from the closed position, should be about correct.